Jerry Campbell was born and raised poor in a large family in the Appalachian Mountains near Hazard, Kentucky. However, he became rich toward God because his mother taught him about the Bible in his youth. His mother gave him his strong faith and love for his living Jehovah God, and when we believe and love God, He also becomes our Heavenly Father.

Jerry has written two books which chronicle his lifelong relationship with God—*The Lake of Fire Is Real and Here on Earth* and *My Guardian Angel Visits*. These books are his testimonial witness of our living Jehovah God, Jesus Christ, and angels.

I would like to dedicate this book to my living Jehovah God, whom I have had a lifelong relationship with. God heard my silent crying prayers at the age of seven when I was at the point of death with chicken pox, measles, and mumps with very high temperature. God sent my guardian angel from heaven and he healed me completely and took my spirit high above my home where I lay in bed in the winter of 1950 and showed me in a 2020 vision the actual Lake of Fire that God will send from out of the heavens at the end of time. God made me both an eye and ear witness to this event.

This is what I saw: the flames were about 100 feet high over the whole Earth where I lived on Browns Fork Kentucky which is near Hazard, KY. And they were burning with a creamy white color with yellow color at the edges of the flames, and black smoke was ascending off the flames going up into the heavens. When I looked up into the heavens, I began to cry because the smoke was so silky black, the whole heaven was total darkness. Then I heard two women near the middle of the 7-acre field we planted every year. One woman said she was a good woman never doing anything bad her whole life and she didn't know why God put her in here, but she never went to Church and serve Him. The other woman said, "Well I am like you, but before God did this to Earth, I had plenty of wealth, but I am so hot and miserable in these flames I would give all my wealth for just one glass of water."

When I awoke the next morning, I was completely healed and there was not any sign of the chicken pox, measles, and mumps on my body. My temperature was gone, but my whole bed was wet where I sweated out my fever. If I owned the whole world and everything therein and gave it all to my wonderful living God, even this would not repay the debt I owe Him.

Jerry Campbell

UNDERSTANDING OUR LIVING JEHOVAH GOD

AUSTIN MACAULEY PUBLISHERS™

LONDON • CAMBRIDGE • NEW YORK • SHARJAH

Ordering Information
Quantity sales: Special discounts are available on quantity purchases by corporations, associations, and others. For details, contact the publisher at the address below.

Publisher's Cataloging-in-Publication data
Campbell, Jerry
Understanding Our Living Jehovah God

ISBN 9781645752592 (Paperback)
ISBN 9781645752585 (Hardback)
ISBN 9781645752608 (ePub e-book)

Library of Congress Control Number: 2021907786

www.austinmacauley.com/us

First Published (2021)
Austin Macauley Publishers LLC
40 Wall Street, 33rd Floor, Suite 3302
New York, NY 10005
USA

mail-usa@austinmacauley.com
+1 (646) 5125767

Introduction

The book is easy to understand, even a young person can learn about God. You will learn mankind came from God, in the story of the creation. How God made us in his image and likeness, putting our eternal spirit inside our mortal bodies and we will live forever in heaven or the Lake of Fire, upon the death of our bodies. You will learn how Adam and Eve fell from the grace of God's plan for them, in the Garden of Eden and learn the truth of how destructive Satan has been for all of mankind.

You will learn the nature of our living Jehovah God and what He requires from mankind to save their spirits, which are our souls in paradise at our death and the New Heaven and New Earth at the end of earth time. You will learn from the Characteristics of God, how that He is the Father of Mankind, by and through the creation of mankind. Our characteristics mirror the likeness of our living God. He has the five senses that He gave us, we have the same feelings as God has, and He also loves what is right and proper and hates things that are wrong and evil, just as we do. You will learn what God requires from mankind to be saved and live in heaven when we die.

You will learn the secret of how Jehovah God is omnipresent, whereby He can be in every place in heaven and on earth at the same time. You will learn the importance of God being omnipotent, whereby He possesses unlimited power and authority over everyone in heaven and on earth. And you will learn how God is omniscience, whereby He knows everything in the past, present, and future.

You will learn why God answers some prayers and no other prayers because they are not His will or there is something wrong with the request. You will learn why bad things happen to some people and good things happen to other people. You will learn why God had to make a place for the evil and wicked people called Hell and the Lake of Fire. And a place for the righteous and good people called Paradise and the New Heaven and New Earth. You will learn of the benefits for serving our living God; we would give the whole world for Him to save our soul from eternal punishment.

You will learn what your eternal life will be like living in heaven or our eternal life will be like living in the Lake of Fire. You will learn how important the spirit of God and Christ is to our lives today. You will determine how important He is to the Christian today on earth, and you will learn all the secrets of how He works on Earth today. You will learn the Holy Spirit is the third person in the Godhead, and how we can commit blasphemy against the Holy Spirit today. Which is the unforgivable sin we can engage, where there is no forgiveness in this world or the world to come? You will learn of God's warnings against committing this sin.

Foreword

Jerry was born on Browns Fork Kentucky, which is three miles from Hazard, Kentucky into a prominent family of ten children. His mother had a significant influence in His life, she was a Christian mother, and she taught him the Scriptures from his youth, beginning at the age of six years old. Therefore, his mother taught Jerry to love his Creator, and she gave him great faith in our living God. Even when Jerry was a prodigal son of God, he always kept his faith and love for God, and when he became a Christian at the age of forty, he has served God these past thirty-five years.

Jerry is highly qualified to write this book, because of his long and personal relationship with his God, from the age of six years old until the present generation of seventy-five years old. Jerry is the only recorded modern day person to be made an eye and ear witness to the Lake of Fire in a vision and to receive a personal visit by his guardian angel from heaven. Jerry communicated with God and Jesus for about thirty minutes through the angel. Jerry has written two books telling these events that took place in his life, title: *The Lake of Fire Is Real and Here on Earth* and *My Guardian Angel Visits* published by West Bow Press.

This book will answer all the questions you have about your life, such as where did I come from? What is the purpose of my life? Why does God allow bad things to happen to people? How does God know everything about my entire life? What must I do to save my soul and go to heaven? Why does God have a place called hell and the Lake of Fire? What does the spirit of God do here on earth today? What will happen when Jesus comes back to earth again? This book will give you faith and confidence in yourself, knowing that God loves you and wants you to be saved and go to heaven to live forever with him and Jesus, with all your family and friends who have loved and kept the commandments of God. You will learn how beautiful life will be, living forever in the New Heaven and New Earth.

Prologue

This book will keep you spellbound because of Jerry's long relationship with our living God. This unique relationship started when Jerry was only six years old when his mother would sit him down and read everything written in the Holy Scriptures about Hell and the Lake of Fire. Our living God must have been listening to his Christian mother read the Bible and God must have loved Jerry's questions and answers he shared with his mother about the Scriptures.

When God sent his Holy Angel, which is Jerry's guardian angel from heaven to visit with him, Jerry communicated with Jehovah God and Jesus Christ through the angel. Jerry learned many things from God, because of this visit; God knew everything about Jerry's entire life, even the secret stuff. God knew every prayer that Jerry made to Him, even the silent prayers. Jerry learned in baptism, God forgave him of all his sins and wrote his name in the book of life in heaven. But when He committed sins and never repented God took his name out of the book of life, but when Jerry repented of the crimes through the angel, God forgave him of that sin and also a sin where Jerry worried about from time to time and sin Jerry did that God didn't think Jerry knew it was a sin. Jerry loved and believed in God, beginning at the age of five years old, and He loved him all his life, even when he sinned. And Jerry learned that God also loved him in return and God had great mercy and great love for Jerry.

When Jerry stood before the angel, communicating with Jehovah God in heaven, God asked him many questions that are all written in Jerry's book he wrote concerning this event. Jerry demonstrated his knowledge of the Holy Bible during this event; because when God had completed his visit with Him, Jerry said to God that he wanted to write a book concerning this visit and the angel said to God, we don't want Jerry writing for us, do we? Jerry knew the Angel thought He was talking about writing a gospel, so Jerry chided into the conversation and explained that He was talking about writing a storybook, which Christians have thousands of books written about their faith and the bookstores are full of them. Then God paid Jerry the highest praise ever received in this life; when God said through the angel, Jerry knows about as much as any man that ever lived about how things are now and how things are going to be. He can write a book. The more Jerry pondered this complement in his heart, he knew that God was always right, he realized how much confusion that people have about his beloved living God, and this qualifies Jerry to write this story in simple and easy to understand form, which everyone can understand the things of God.

Chapter One

The Origin of Mankind

We know someone made everything on earth and it stands to reason, mankind was created in the beginning by someone. And our maker was Jehovah God, who has eyes to see with, nose to smell with, ears to hear with, hands to feel with, and legs to walk. God has a spirit which is the Holy Ghost, and he has a mind filled with intelligence which is above all in heaven and on the earth. God is the beginning of all things in heaven and on the earth, even all the stars and planets in the heavens.

All the other Gods made with wood, stone, or metal, and they have eyes, but don't see, have ears, but don't hear, nose, but don't smell, hands, but don't feel, legs, but don't walk. These Gods are hollow inside, and they don't have the power of intelligence, having no heart, mind, or soul.

God lived in heaven at the beginning of His creation, created His son, Jesus Christ, in His express image. God made Jesus a member of the Godhead with Himself and God's Holy Spirit and everything built in heaven and on earth was created through, by, and for His son. Then God created all the angels in heaven with the intent that everyone lives there together for all eternity. God is a spirit person, and when He made mankind, God created an outward man and called it our body and God made the inner man and called it our spirit, which is in the express image of our God Jehovah in heaven.

Then God made the heavens, which is all the planets and stars in the heavens where God and all the hosts of heaven live. God created the Earth at first, covered entirely with water, and according to scientists, the earth is six hundred billion years old, using carbon dating to gauge the age of the earth. When God first created the earth, He put the earth full of minerals, precious stones, oil, gas, diamonds, gold, iron, salt, coal, and many other such things did God put inside the earth for mankind's future usage. Only a father that loves his children would give them such great gifts. The earth was without form, and it was dark continually on the earth, then the spirit of God moved upon the face of the waters, and it was God's Holy Spirit that did the work.

God swung into action, He created the sun to rule over the day, and He divided the light from the darkness. God made the moon, which rules over the night, and God called the light *day* and the darkness *night*. God said let this be for a sign, and for seasons, and for days and years. God gave mankind four seasons; spring, summer, fall, and winter, and according to a scientist, the earth's temperature has never changed from the creation of the earth more or less than two percentage points in degrees hotter or colder.

Then God made the skies, which He called the firmament, to separate the waters that were on the earth from the waters that God made above the heavens, for mankind's benefit of rain coming from the skies to water the crops and all the Earth. God shows his great love for mankind in the creation, which is self-evident of God's motives for creating all the things of the earth. We take for granted these great enjoyments that God gave us in His creation, but mankind could not exist without them.

God said to the spirit, let there be mountains in the midst of the waters of the earth to divide the waters from the earth, and God called the waters Seas and called the dry land, Earth. Then God gave mankind his endless supply of food, to harvest from the earth. Everything that God created on earth He put the seed to reproduce again after its kind, for the food supply of all mankind, as long as time endures on earth. God made all the grass, all the trees, all the vegetables, and all the fruits, and trees, with the seed within itself to come again upon the earth, after its own kind.

Then God created every creature that is upon the Earth and living in the Seas. God made the seas to bring forth every living creature of the Seas in great abundance. Then God created every residing bird and fowls that fly above the earth in the atmosphere of the skies. God said to the creatures, be fruitful and multiply and fill the waters of the seas, and the fouls increase upon the earth.

Now it was the sixth day of God's creation, and God went into overdrive so that he could finish his work of all His creation by the end of this day. God created every living creature from the dust of the earth. And he put the seed inside of every male creature that God made upon the earth, all cattle, every beast, and everything that creeps upon the earth. God did not make any of the animals or creatures, in his image by giving them a spirit; therefore, He does not require their spirit back upon their death, nor to stand before

Him in judgment. They die and return to the dust of the earth from where they came from in God's creation.

For out of the ground, after God formed every beast of the field and every fowl of the air, God brought them all to Adam to see what He would call them, and what Adam chose to call them, which was their name unto this day. Now this same living God Jehovah, He knew how to talk and when He made Adam and Eve, God also gave them the intelligence and power to speak a language, from the beginning of time.

And, then God said to Jesus Christ, who sits on the throne next to God's throne in heaven, "Let us create man, in our image, after our likeness."

Therefore, after God formed man from the dust of the ground, God made man in his express image when He put man's spirit in his body and breathed the breath of life into his nostrils. Humanity has a spirit that is eternal, and no one can kill our spirit except God. And God gave man to have dominion over everything that we have created. Then God said to Jesus Christ; it is not right that man should be alone; I will make him a helper. And God caused Adam to fall into a deep sleep and God took a rib out of Adams side, closing up the flesh of Adam, and God made Adam; a woman to be his wife and brought her to Adam. Then Adam said, "She is bone of my bones, and flesh of my flesh, I will call woman because she came from man. Therefore, shall a man leave his father and mother, and shall cleave unto his wife, and they shall be one flesh."

They were both naked, the man and his wife, and were not ashamed. God put the seed in the man to reproduce

16

another human being after his image and likeness again, to replenish the earth.

Now God shows his great love for his creation of mankind, God planted for them a garden eastward in Eden, and he put them in the garden. God made every tree to grow in the garden that was pleasant to the eye for food. God planted the tree of life there also, and the tree of knowledge of good and evil. And God commanded the man that they could eat of every tree in the garden, except the tree of knowledge of good and evil, you shall not eat of it: for in the day that you eat thereof, you shalt surely die.

God showed his great love toward mankind, even in the creation. If Adam and Eve could only obey God's one commandment, they could live forever in the magnificent garden that God planted and made for them to eat. But Satan enticed Eve to eat of the fruit from the tree of knowledge of knowing to do Good and to do evil which God commanded not to eat of this tree.

Therefore, when God made Adam and Eve, he gave them a spirit, which is called their ghost that comes forth from their bodies at their death. Our spirits are in the express image of our living Jehovah God, and He requires it back at our departure. Those of us that have loved God and kept His commandments our spirits will go to heaven when we die, but those of us that do not love Jehovah God and obey his commandments. When they die, God will send the angel of death for them, and he will put their ghost in hell with Satan and all the lost souls.

Since mankind came from the creation of our living Jehovah God, this makes this same God, the father of all mankind upon the earth, even though our biological fathers are of the earth, they are our earthly fathers; but God is our heavenly father.

God made all the hosts of heaven, and He made them with a celestial body, which is a heavenly body that does not possess flesh and blood. God did not cause them to reproduce and multiply after their kind in heaven; because God made them to live forever in heaven. They never die or get sick, never are in need of anything that God does not furnish them freely with love. They neither labor nor toil for their living, such as mankind does.

The longevity of the lives of Adam and his family makes it self-evident that God intended at Creation they should live forever in the Garden of Eden. Adam lived nine hundred and thirty years, Adam's son, Seth, lived nine hundred and twelve years, and E'nos lived nine hundred and five years. Ca-I-nan lived nine hundred and ten years; Mahalaleel lived eight hundred and ninety-five years. Jared lived nine hundred and sixty-two years, Methuselah was the oldest man ever to live on earth and he lived to be nine hundred and sixty-nine years old and he died.

God made all mankind with a terrestrial body, and all mankind upon the earth has the same kind of flesh and the same type of blood in their bodies. These bodies God made for us, they get sick, and they will die at various ages. God created our bodies to reproduce to replenish the earth with humans. But we can be of good cheer and God made us humans to have the inward mankind with a spirit, whereas when we die our inner mankind comes out of our bodies and goes back to our living God who gave every human being a spirit. According to doctor studies and test at the exact time of our death, we lose two ounces of weight and that is what our spirit weighs, it departs out of our bodies at our departure.

The key to knowledge to understanding our living Jehovah God, we must realize where mankind first came from a god that was intelligent and living who possessed the knowledge and power to create us. We must accept the fact that a mere monkey or ape, does not own the intelligence, or the capability to produce us humans, and they are still in cages at zoos. No animal has the knowledge and abilities of humans. For you to understand our living God, you must first accept his holy scriptures known as the Holy Bible. You must have faith in Jehovah God to please Him because anyone that comes to God to serve Him must believe that He is God and a rewarder of all who diligently seek Him. The Holy Ghost gave Apostle Luke the genealogy tracing Jesus Christ's earthly father, Joseph, all the way back to Adam and Jehovah God in heaven.

Chapter Two

The Original Sin of Mankind

Adam and Eve were living in the beautiful garden in Eden, where God had planted them the perfect garden. God made every tree pleasant to the eye and good for food, God made a great river that runs through the garden that furnished the water for the trees and herbs. When the river passed through the garden, it parted into four heads of four different rivers.

There had been a great war in heaven, because Satan, whose name is Lucifer, became envious and jealous of Jehovah God. Satan desired in his heart to ascend into heaven, higher than God, He wanted to sit on a throne, ruling over the congregation, on the north side of heaven. Satan wished to emulate our living Jehovah God. There was one-third of the angels in heaven followed Satan in his plot to overthrow the power of Jehovah God. But Jesus Christ and the other two-thirds of the angels left who wanted to continue serving God, they overcame Satan and his angels and God threw them out of heaven down to Earth.

At that time the serpent was the most mentally keen animal upon the earth, and he was first created to walk in an upright position on two feet. The serpent must have been pleasant to the eye, and the serpent was very deceitful in his dealings with Eve. All of God's angels are very powerful, and they can become invisible or visible, having no flesh and bones as humans have. So Satan entered into the serpent and he communicated with Eve from the inner parts of serpent.

Satan only changed one word in the commandment of God to Eve. God Commanded that they could eat of every tree in the Garden; but the tree in the middle of the garden, which God called the tree of knowledge of good and evil. God said in the day that you eat from this tree, you shall surely die. Satan quoted God; but added just one word, Satan told Eve, you shall not surely die; because in that day, God knows that your eyes will be opened and you will know good and evil. Eve believed Satan, and she saw that the fruit on the tree of knowledge was pleasant to the eye and good for food, a tree she desired to make her wise, and she ate of the forbidden fruit and gave her husband, Adam, to eat of the fruit, and he did eat.

Here is the first sin that was committed by mankind and when our living God asked Adam, what have you done? And Adam blamed his wife for giving him the fruit to eat, and when God asked Eve, "What have you done?"

She blamed Satan for breaking the commandment, saying to God, "The serpent deceived and lied to me and I did eat."

They condemned others for their sin; but this did not work with God. He held each one of them accountable for their crimes.

From the first sin that on the earth, shows us the severity of His sentence of punishment for our crimes that we commit, down through the history of all mankind. God executed his judgment upon the serpent; first, God said, "Because you have done this, cursed above the cattle and every beast of the earth, you shall crawl upon your belly and eat dust all the days of your life. And I will put an enemy between you and your seeds and Eve and her seeds."

Then God executed his judgment upon Eve. Next, God said He would significantly increase Eve's sorrows and she would conceive and bring forth children, her desire would be to her husband and he would rule over her. Eve fell from having eternal life here on earth and living in the beautiful garden that our living God made for Eve. God had given Eve everything in her life that she could desire to have if she would obey this one commandment. Now Eve would become a keeper of the home, having children, teaching them good things in life. God made Eve the weaker vessel, but her duties in life are mighty hard to perform because a woman's work is hard.

Now God came to Adam, to pass His judgment on Adam for his sin, and it was also very severe. Because Adam did not have to work for his living, God gave him everything He would need freely in the garden of eternal life. Now God said to Adam because you have obeyed the voice of your wife and eaten of the tree, that I commanded you not to eat from this tree. God saying, "Cursed is the ground for your sake, in sorrow, you shall eat from the ground all the days of your life. Thorns and Thistles shall the land bring forth and you shall eat the herb of the field; you will work all the days of your life by the sweat of your face. You will eat bread until you return unto the ground; for out of it you were taken, dust you are and dust you shall return."

God loved them; still He made the clothing for their naked bodies, and then he expelled them out of the Garden of Eden. Then God said to Jesus Christ, "Look, they have become as one of us, to know good and evil: and now they may put forth their hand and also eat of the tree of life and live forever."

So God expelled them from the Garden of Eden, and God sent two angels with flaming swords to guard the tree of life, preventing them from eating of the eternal fruit from the tree.

Satan was the very first person to tell a lie and this makes him the father of lies. Satan was the first person to commit murder when he lied to Eve in quoting the word of God when he added a single word to the commandment that God gave Adam and Eve about forbidding them to eat fruit from the tree of knowledge. Satan became the original murderer of Eve and Adam; because now God took the tree of life from them, making them mortal because someday they would suffer the death of their bodies.

From the beginning of time, Satan has misused the scriptures of God, and he seeks the ruin of all mankind. Satan is the father of all evil, afflictions, diseases, and he incites mankind to sin. Satan blinds the minds of unbelievers, so the word of God does not shine into their hearts.

The key of knowledge to understanding our living Jehovah God and Satan, who is the God of this world, is to know their character. Jehovah God loves righteousness and He hates evil, but Satan loves evil and hates righteousness. Jehovah God wants everyone to be saved and spend eternity in the New Earth and New Heaven, but Satan wants everyone to be lost and spend eternity with him in Hell and the Lake of Fire at the end of time.

Chapter Three

The Father of Evil and Death
Is Satan

The key to understanding why Jehovah God operates in heaven and on earth is to know how the God of this world, which is Satan, operates his kingdom.

Satan became the father of all evil; because he was the beginning of evil when He rebelled and Rioted against Jehovah God in heaven. When he came to earth, there was just Adam and Eve living on earth for all eternity. Then Satan became the father of lies when he told Eve the first lie ever told on earth, and he became the father of murder when he told eve, she would surely not die when she ate of the forbidden fruit from the tree of life God planted in the middle of the Garden of Eden. So when Eve obeyed Satan instead of Jehovah God, he passed judgment on the sin of Adam and Eve. God revoked His original plan of eternal life for Adam and Eve, making them mortal. Therefore, their bodies would not live forever on Earth, but their bodies would die, making Satan the father of murder, because he was the first murderer.

Satan had great power when Jesus came to earth, He could give Jesus all the kingdoms of this world if He would fall and worship Him, but Jesus did not accept his offer. Satan is the tempter of all mankind to commit evil acts on this Earth; but Jehovah God does not tempt, and when Satan tempts mankind, God will make way for you to escape the snare of the devil's trap. When Satan tempted Jesus, Satan did quote some scriptures correctly, but He misapplied them and Jesus would merely quote the scriptures of God that applied to the situation at hand. When the devil wanted Jesus to worship him, Jesus said, "Get behind me, Satan; for it is written, you shall worship the Lord, thy God, and Him only shall you serve."

We can see here that when Satan could not entice Jesus to serve him, Satan wanted Jesus to jump off the highest point of the temple wall at Jerusalem and kill himself.

People on earth when they do not resist the power of Satan, they become his servant and commit all manner of evil. When people do evil things, they have Satan living in their bodies and controlling them; this makes everyone who commit crimes the children of Satan. And the children of Satan will commit these crimes. All manner of murders, blasphemers of God, homosexuality, drunkards, sexual immorality, liar's, denying God, those who change the word of God to suit themselves. All who have foolish imaginations, false worship, haters of God, rioters without love in their hearts, disobey their parents. They are full of malignity against other people, full of debating God's word, full of extortion, having no self-control, having no mercy for others, having no honor for anyone. They are without understanding, professing themselves to be wise, they have become fools.

There was a particular man who lived in the Country of Gadarenes, who was full of devils, so much that they drove him crazy. The town folks had to put him in chains, and he lived in the city graveyard among the tombs. But when Jesus came into his country, he cast out the devils, and this man became back into his right mind. When the people of the town heard what had happened, they went out to see for themselves, and they found this crazy man, clothed, in his right mind, sitting at Jesus's feet, worshipping him. Today, that when we give Satan place in our lives and hearts, he will drive us crazy with his tricks and enticements, to induce us to commit sins against God. But when we believe in the son of God and allow Jesus into our minds and hearts, we, too, will be in our right mind, going to church and worshipping Jesus also.

After fifteen hundred and fifty-six years of mankind living on the earth with Satan, it came to pass that Satan had corrupted all the people upon the earth. Their minds and hearts filled with violence and corruption. The God of heaven said my spirit will not always strive with mankind, yet will I give him one hundred and twenty years to repent and turn from their sins. Then God said, "I will destroy both mankind and every beast and creeping thing, and all the fouls of the air; because it repenteth me that I have made them."

But God looked down from heaven, and He saw Noah and his three sons, Shem, Ham, and Japheth, and their wives all walking with God. Then God spoke to Noah and gave him instructions how to build an ark to save the eight souls from death and two of every living thing upon the earth, one male and one female, to repopulate the earth.

Satan walks around on earth, looking for anyone that he can persuade to commit an offense against their fellow mankind and Jehovah God. Satan entices mankind to commit sexual immorality through the lust of our flesh by tempting the weak in the flesh, to act on their desires created by Satan. Sin can produce poverty and ruin of our lives by becoming a drunkard from alcohol or drugs, Satan enslaves the will of mankind by the power of these drugs, which produce many miseries upon this earth for mankind. Satan uses the sins of hatred, division, and racism to harden mankind's hearts against their fellow mankind, filling their hearts with hatred for one another. Satan uses abortion of children in their mother's womb to murder their flesh and blood. Satan is working overtime in America; look at all the hatred, murders, robberies, raping, drunkards, broken homes, and lives caused by our sins. Satan is the God of all the evil and death in this world, which was and is now and is to come, until the end of time.

God set the choice of life and good or death and evil, before mankind and gave us the freedom to choose the way in life that we decide to go here on earth. Many have adopted the broad highway that leads to evil and death, sending our Souls to Hell when we die. Few have chosen the narrow road that leads to good and life, which addresses our souls to heaven when we die. The wages of sin is death, but the gift of God is eternal life.

The humankind, who wishes to go to heaven when they die, must not get on the long black train to ride through their lifetime on earth. This train is black from the sin's that those

28

who have committed here on earth. This train is full of the darkness of the passenger's sins and its destination is bound for death and hell. They have allowed Satan to take control of their lives and he is their engineer of the train.

There is one thing that our Living God hates and that is sin's that mankind commits against one another, which is an offense against God. When Satan and one-third of the angels in heaven followed Satan in an attempt to overthrow the power of God, He prepared a special place for them and all mankind that would also support the sins of Satan and called it hell. God had no choice but to protect Himself from Satan; therefore, Satan is the father of hell because he was the beginning of hell.

The key of knowledge to understanding why bad things happen to people is all written in the Holy Bible. Jehovah God is responsible for everything that is righteous and good in our lives. God is full of love and mercy for his children, and it is his good pleasure to give them all good things in their lives. But Satan is full of hatred and evil for all mankind, he is our enemy, always seeking out those whom he can devour by committing wrongdoing against others. Satan is the first person to sin in heaven and on earth, thus, making him the father of all his children that follow him, who commit sins. Choose this day whom you will serve, the God of life and good, or the god of this world, Satan, and follow the ways of evil and death.

Chapter Four

The Father of Righteousness and Life Is God

Jehovah God is love, He is righteous, and He is full of goodness and mercy for mankind. Let mankind love one another, for God is love, everyone who loves one another here on earth is born of God and knows God. Those who do not like one another have hatred in their hearts, and they do not know God, because God is love. God made known His love for us, in that while we were still sinners, God sent His only begotten son, Jesus Christ, into the world, to die on the cross as the sacrifice for our sins. Herein is love, if God loved us so much, then we should love one another, therein God will live in our bodies, and his love is perfected in us.

You have heard it said how can you love a God who we are supposed to fear? Well, this is easy to understand, you should fear God when you are doing things that God tells us not to do, but we do not fear God when we are doing the things He tells us to obey in the Holy Scriptures. Here is a comparison, the Scriptures say, *"The higher powers that are ordained of God and when we break the Laws of our Land, we should be afraid of the Law; But if we obey the*

Laws of our Land, we should not be scared because we will have the praise of the police."

In the days of old time, we feared our earthly fathers when we did not obey their word, for we knew he would whip us with a belt or big switch. But when we followed his word, we did not fear him, because he loved us so much and would do any thing he could for us. He worked and supplied us with a home, food, and clothing. This is why the Scriptures say, *"Children are to obey their parents who are in the lord and honor our fathers and mothers that we may live long on the earth."*

Jehovah God is Light and in Him is no darkness at all. If we say that we have fellowship with God and walk in the darkness of sins, we lie and do not the truth. But if we walk while living on earth in the light of the gospels of Jesus Christ, we will have fellowship with God and the blood of Jesus Christ, His son, cleanses us from all our sins. When the rich young ruler of the Jews asked Jesus Christ this question, "Good Master, what good thing may I do, to inherit eternal life?"

Did Jesus say to him, "Why call me 'Good'? There is none good, except God."

Jehovah God is good all the time, His thoughts are not like that of mankind, and His ways are not like the ways of mankind. God's thoughts and ideas are always higher than mankind. God is holy all the time, and God is Righteous all the time, God's heart is full of love and mercy for mankind all the time. God is not a respecter of persons, He loves all people of all races of His creation, He loves the yellow, black, red, and white people and they all are precious in His sight. God created them all in his likeness and image. God is not willing that any of His children should be lost, but that all should come to repentance of their sins and be saved.

Every good and perfect gift mankind receives upon this earth comes from our living father of life, and with God, there is no changing, nor even a shadow of Him turning from His great love for us. God forms us in our mother's womb, He names every one of us with an everlasting name, and He numbers every hair on our heads when He appoints our lifespan on earth. In God we move and have our being, we are the offsprings of God. Children are a blessing from God, and they are God's heritage. God gives every one of us specific talents and individual abilities, which we will possess from our mother's womb. So, everyone that is born, God has a particular purpose for us. God gives us our fruits and vegetables and our meats, and He supplies us with all our needs upon the earth. God gave us living waters in the form of rain, whereas our natural bodies will not perish from the earth, due to thirst, all the days of our lives. Also, God gave us eternal living waters, and when mankind partakes of these waters, they will never thirst again; because these waters that Jesus give us will be in us a well of water springing up into everlasting life. When you accept God's Plan of Salvation of our souls, we are baptized into the waters that give us eternal life. If we remain faithful unto our end, we will receive eternal life in heaven, where we can drink living waters that flow from the throne of God in heaven.

God gives us our seasons; springtime, summertime, fall time, winter time, and God gave them for mankind to measure days and years. God made heaven, earth, and the sea, and all things that are therein. Therefore, God left mankind a witness of Himself, in that God did good and gave us rain from heaven, and very fruitful seasons, filling mankind's hearts with food and gladness. The living Jehovah God; He loves His creation, especially mankind; because He made us in His express image and likeness. Therefore, God will never suffer His laws of maintaining nature to get out of control, of becoming too hot or too cold for mankind to reproduce His food to nourish their bodies for growth and life while here on earth. Our God will supply all our needs according to His riches in glory by Jesus Christ in these last times.

God also gives His children that partake of the living waters, being born again into the Kingdom of God, a brand-new heart being likeminded as Jesus Christ. Who was full of love and mercy for others, and took upon himself the form of a servant in helping other people and He esteemed others more than He did Himself. Jesus never tried to build himself any reputation but took upon himself the form of a servant. When you are born again, God will give you the gift of the Holy Spirit which will live in your body and help you with your prayers to God, and your physical or moral infirmities. The Holy Spirit will be your witness before God, He will give you the wisdom of the Holy Scriptures, He will be your guide in your life, and He will lead you besides the calmness of this life on earth who will give you sweet sleep and rest. The Holy Spirit will guide you in the paths of righteousness; all who are led by the spirit are the Sons and daughters of God. If we die with the Holy Spirit of God living in our mortal bodies, this same spirit who raised Jesus up from the dead will also raise our human bodies by the spirit that lives in us.

God also gives His children the power over all the power of Satan and his demons; we can rejoice that our names are written in the Book of Life in heaven. Christians today can resist Satan and his demons, and they will flee from them. God will restore our soul; if we commit a sin, when we repent and pray to God for forgiveness with a sorrowful heart and have the church or righteous people pray to God on our behalf to forgive our sin, God will forgive you and restore you into the Book of Life in heaven. God is full of mercy for all who show mercy toward others on earth.

Jesus Christ told his disciples when they saw him; they saw his father; because God was in him and the words that he spoke were the words of his father. In the last dispensation of time, God has spoken to mankind by His son, Jesus Christ. God loved mankind so much that he sent Jesus to offer salvation to all mankind. Jesus brought a New Covenant of truth to Mankind, and Jesus showed us the way we can get to heaven in the New Covenant, and God offered us Eternal Life in His son, Jesus Christ. Jehovah God is the source of all Grace, which He offered Mankind in the New Covenant. When we are first saved, we are saved by grace and not by our works; because we had no works, only faith. We are kept saved by our faith and our works, which Jesus will bring into our judgment. God declares that the wages of sin is death, but the gift of God is eternal life through Jesus Christ our lord. Well, we can't earn eternal life; but we must run the race like apostle Paul did, giving it our one hundred percent effort, and love God and keep his commandments.

The key of knowledge to understanding the goodness of Jehovah God is on this wise. God created all the angels in heaven to live in heaven, but Satan messed up that plan. God created man to live for eternity in the Garden of Eden that He planted Himself, but Satan messed up that plan. Satan is the father of all evil and hell and the Lake of Fire was made for him and all his children. God's Goodness is on this wise; He created a New Heaven and New Earth where all his angels, saints, and Christians will live for all eternity. We will live in comfort, peace, never die, never get sick, never thirst or hunger, everyone loves one another, and all live together, we will rest from our labors, enjoying life forever and ever, living in mansions and walking on streets made with pure gold. Everyone will be equal to the angels in heaven.

Chapter Five

God's Requirement for Mankind's Salvation

Jehovah God requires all who hear the word of God, and they believe the words from God that is delivered unto them through His holy prophets, His son, Jesus Christ, and His apostles, that is written in the Holy Bible. Then God requires that they are born again of water and they must live faithfully until their death to be saved and go live in heaven for eternity. This is the law of admission into the Kingdom of God, which is the church that Jesus Christ built here on earth for his Father God.

Since God made the heavens and earth and everything therein, and He created us with so much love in His heart, that He requires us to love Him in return. You can compare the feelings of God with the sentiments of our Earthly Father who demands His children love Him and obey Him. This is why Jehovah God said through the mouth of His son, Jesus Christ, that mankind was to love the Lord, their God, with all their heart, and with all their soul, and with their entire mind. This is the first and highest law from our Living God to mankind and the second is like unto it, that we shall love our neighbor as we love ourselves. On these two commandments from God, hang all the law and the prophets.

This is my testimony of why I love Jehovah God. At the age of six years old, my mother would sit me down and read to me all the Scriptures about hell. She was a good Christian and went to church every Sunday and served God. My mother was a good keeper of our home, while my father was a good provider for his family, working. I believed in God, because my mother believed and was an excellent example to me, and I loved God because He loved the beggar man named Lazarus. This story in the Scriptures made me think, *What a great God my mother serves, He loves poor people and my family is poor.*

God must have liked my mother, and He must have been listening to my questions and answers that I asked my mother during our Bible readings about hell. Because when I was seven years old, in the middle of the winter of 1950, I came down with chickenpox, measles, and mumps all within two days with a temperature of about 107 degrees.

My earthly father and mother thought that it was my last days on this earth; they did not have the money to take me to Hazard, Kentucky to see a doctor who might have saved me. Sitting around the fireplace, it occurred to me that I would not live to see tomorrow. With tears streaming my face, I pulled the covers back and looked at the backs of their heads. And my mother was crying and told the other children to quit complaining about Jerry getting all the covers, except one for each bed in the house and she said that my father was upset because if we had the money, we could take Jerry to Hazard to the doctors and probably save him. So I lay back down with rivers of tears running down my face and I thought how sad, no one on this earth can save me.

As I laid there crying, it suddenly occurred to me, I know someone who can save me, it is God, He can do anything, He made everything, and God loves poor people, and I am dirt poor. So I prayed to God three times because I had to have an answer that night or I would not live to see tomorrow. On the third time, I made a deal with God; my prayer was on this wise, "Dear God, I am just a little boy, I am too young to die, I don't want to die. I want to make a deal with you, if you will heal me and let me live to be an old man, I will do so something that you will be very proud of me for doing, I don't know what, but I will do something. If you don't take my deal and I die tonight, you got to bring me to heaven; because I have not sinned. Now you answer me in the name of Jesus Christ."

No answer came at first, and I said, "Well, it is okay. If you don't want to answer me, I know you are there, and I believe in you; because my mother has been teaching me the bible and I love you; because you loved poor people and saved Lazarus and I am poor."

I testify before heaven and Earth, as I lay there this voice of an old man came to me inside my head, and God said, "Little boy, why are you crying? Look again, these same people that you see tonight, you will see again tomorrow when you awaken." In a louder voice, He said, "Now lay down and go to sleep!"

Well, He said to look again at my family around the fireplace, so I did and as I lay back down, pulling the covers over my head, and going into a deep sleep. That night God sent my guardian angel from heaven (who spoke to me the words that God told him to speak, as I learned when He visited me in 2011.)

God's angel took my spirit high above my home on Browns Fork Kentucky and showed me the actual lake of fire that is coming upon the earth at the last day. Also, I heard two women coming across the seven-acre field we planted every year and they were complaining how hot and miserable they were in these flames. The wealthy woman would have given her entire fortune for one glass of water!

Here is what the Lake of Fire looked like to me, from high above the flames. It was the strangest fire that I ever saw in this vision. There is no fire like it upon the earth, the fire was approximately 100 feet high and the color of the flames was a creamy white color with yellow color at the edges of the fire and black smoke was ascending up from the fire into the heavens. When I looked at the mountains on each side of the field, where I lived on earth, I could tell the outline of the flames on the mountains was higher than those down in the valley in the area. Black smoke was ascending up into the heavens from them and as I looked into the heavens, it was as silky black. And there were no stars, sun, moon or any planets in the skies, and then I began to cry and said to myself, "I thought God was going to take my deal, He has let me die and go to Hell."

Then it was like someone shook me and when I awaken, I was 100% cured, not a sign or trace of the diseases was visible on my body.

I love Jehovah God more than I love anyone in heaven or on earth because He saved my life more than once during my seventy-five years. God Himself has written my name down in the Book of Live in heaven. Jehovah God sent my guardian angel to visit me in 2011, and I communicated with God and Jesus Christ in heaven through God's angel. My two books, title, *The Lake of Fire Is Real and Here on Earth* and *My Guardian Angel Visits* by Jerry Campbell. God gave me, my wife, and children, and *my* ability to earn a living, good health and long life. The Guardian Angel said, "God loved me so much, He has been so good to me all the days of my life, even when I did not deserve it. No one in heaven or earth has more love or faith in God than me."

Jehovah God requires of mankind; we worship Him in spirit and truth. God, in the beginning, set aside Saturday as the holy day to worship Him; but when He sent Jesus Christ into the world, to make a new covenant with mankind, God set aside the day to worship Him on Sunday. Jehovah God is a jealous God, if we put anything before worshipping Him, God will visit the sin of the fathers upon their children, even down through the generations of them that hate God. But God will show great mercy unto all the people that worship Him and keep His commandments. God warns mankind in the New Testament, not to forsake going to church on Sundays to worship Him, for in doing so, we commit a willful sin against God. When we drop out of going to church on Sundays, the blood of Jesus Christ does not remain to wash away your sins. You have nothing to look forward to, but your judgment and fiery indignation, which shall devour the adversaries of Jehovah God.

Now I will testify before all in heaven and upon the earth, when Jehovah God sent my guardian angel to visit me in 2011, God chastised me and rebuked me from heaven,

40

speaking through His holy angel whom He sent. God knew my entire life, He knew every sin that I committed, and He knew every prayer that I made to Him in heaven, even the silent prayers. As I stood before the angel, God knew my very thoughts, and He knew me better than I knew me. When God rebuked me and chastised me for my sins, I repented with a broken heart and tears of remorse and shame. Not only did God forgive the sin He chastised me for; God said through the angel, "Jerry, since you have repented of this sin, God is also going to forgive you of the sin that you worry about from time to time. And even the sin that God doesn't think that you knew sin and He is going to write your name back into the book of life. What do you feel about Jehovah God's mercy?"

As I took inventory of my life, it came to me these two sins' that my blessed father in heaven showed me great mercy in his forgiveness. So God requires mankind to pray to Him, and He treasures all our prayers up in heaven. God expects us to repent of our sins, only then will He show us mercy and forgive us our sins.

God requires Mankind to have faith in Him, for God has said without faith it is impossible to please Him. We must have saving faith, meaning we will believe every word of God written in the Scriptures. We will live our lives according to the commandments written in the Scriptures. This kind of faith will give us good works, whereas we are judged according to our works.

God requires children to obey their parents in the Lord: for this is right. And to honor our fathers and mothers, we will have a long life upon the Earth.

Jehovah God requires all his children who serve Him to repent of their sins when they commit them. God gives us a specific time frame to repent of the sin. If we do not repent, then God will remove our names out of the Book of Life in heaven; but if we repent of the wrongdoing at a later date, then God will forgive us our sin and write our names back into the Book of Life in heaven.

The key to knowledge to understanding the manifold wisdom of our living Jehovah God is to know there is a beginning of mankind on earth. And at the beginning of the last times of earth, God sent His beloved son, Jesus Christ, down from heaven to mediate a new covenant whereby all mankind could have a plan of salvation to save themselves from death and the lake of fire. God has made the church that Jesus built the custodian of the manifold wisdom of God as recorded in the Holy Bible. Therein is recorded the beginning of mankind and God's plan of salvation for us, and how we should live to win the crown of eternal life in heaven. God explains our purpose for having a life to live here on earth, and He explains what our eternal end will be according to the life we live here on earth.

Chapter Six

God's Characteristics Are
Superior to Mankind's

The knowledge of our living Jehovah God surpasses all of the experience of mankind combined. God knows mankind's entire life from our mother's womb to our grave. God knows mankind every thought and intent of their hearts. God knows when just one sparrow falls from the skies. God has every hair upon mankind's heads all numbered, and He also knows when we will drop dead. God knows all the people of the earth, and knows everyone who belongs to Him and serves Him; also knows everyone that belongs to and serves Satan. God knows everything that mankind has in their possessions, and He knows how you got them. God knows all the secrets of mankind's hearts, and there is nothing that we have hidden from God. Because God never forgets the names of people, as we forget sometimes. God knows every prayer that you have ever made to Him in heaven.

The wisdom of our living Jehovah God is beyond measure; but when mankind lacks wisdom, who are His children serving him in the church, all we have to do is pray to God to give us the wisdom to understand certain things, and if we do not doubt, then God will provide us with the wisdom we ask of Him. God has given me the wisdom to understand the Scriptures, comparing spiritual things with spiritual things. God is a liberal giver of wisdom and useful gifts to mankind, and He will help you also. God's wisdom is pure, peaceable, gentle, easy to accept, full of love, mercy, and good fruits, without partiality and without hypocrisy. The wisdom of this world is foolishness with God; for God takes the wise in their craftiness. What man knows the things of another man on earth but the spirit of man which is in him? And no man knows the things of Jehovah God, except the spirit of God, and that spirit lives in Christians. Therefore, the wisdom of Christians is far more significant than the wisdom of the children of the prince of this world, which is Satan; their wisdom is foolishness with Jehovah God.

God loves Mankind so profoundly that it is beyond our comprehension; what person among us would give up their only begotten son to die for the sinners and ungodly people of this world? Who among us would stand by and say nothing when our son was crucified by their enemies, which convicted God's son to suffer the death on the Cross? What would mother among us stand and watch their only son be beaten with forty lashes and watch him carry his cross to the mountaintop where his enemies took long metal spikes and nailed his hands and feet to the Cross? This son's name is Jesus Christ, and his father is Jehovah God from heaven, and his mother is named Mary, she is of the earth. Therefore, Jesus was the son of God and the son of man. This son had not done any evil; he went about the earth just doing well unto all mankind. Now I ask you this question? Who among mankind on earth would die on the Cross for the sinners and ungodly, who were your enemies?

Why did our living God in heaven allow this to happen to His son? Well, God has always since the beginning of time, required a blood sacrifice to cleanse mankind's sins. But in the Old Testament, God used the blood of bulls and goats to wash mankind's sins but it only rolled back the crimes for one year. All mankind who lived and died under the Old Testament had to make atonement for all their sins every year.

Therefore, God sent His only begotten son down from heaven with this mission to accomplish. Jesus would be born from the bloodlines of God's earthly son, Adam, tracing the genealogy of Jesus Christ from Adam all the way down through the generations to Joseph. Jesus would preach the words that God gave him for the new covenant between God and mankind. Jesus would preach the gospel to the poor and He would heal the sick and brokenhearted. He would teach deliverance of the people who were held in captivity by Satan, and He would set them free from the power of darkness and shine the light of life unto them, He would restore the sight of the blind and preach that this is the acceptable year of the Lord. Jesus was sent to mediate the New Covenant by the death on the cross; his blood being used by God to wash away mankind's sins, never to be remembered again by God.

God does not change; He is the same yesterday, today, and tomorrow, forever and ever. God has always loved righteousness and hated evil. God who made all the heavens and the earth are the work of his hands, they shall all perish, but God will remain the same. The angels that sinned in heaven, God threw out of heaven, and Jesus put them in hell to await the final Judgment Day, the people of the old timers who hated God but loved evil, God put all them in hell, God remains the same, he is eternal, He is forever. Jehovah God requires mankind not to change anything written in the Holy Bible. If we change them, we will bring all the plagues written in the Holy Bible upon us for this sin.

Jehovah God is holy, and He is pure, sinless, always right, He has almighty power more enormous than anyone in heaven or earth, God is worthy of mankind's admiration and our worship of Him. There is not but one God and father of all who is, above all and through all and in all Christians. God is holy, and He expects us Christians to be holy also. God never sins, but we do; therefore, we must repent of our sins to remain sacred.

Jehovah God is a Jealous God of His children who serve Him, why? Well, God loves His children, He supplies all their needs, He answers their prayers if there is nothing amiss with the request. He gives His children good gifts, and he gives them His spirit to live in our bodies to help us with our lives here on earth. When mankind who serve Him goes astray, and serves false gods, forsaking the only true living God, Then God becomes jealous because He has lost a son or daughter to a false god.

Jehovah God did not pity the nation of Israel when they turned away from serving Him and started serving pagan false gods. And this brought the judgment of Jehovah God upon the Nation of Israel according to the sins they committed. And God sent His anger upon them, and God repaid them for their abominations, and God did not spare

46

them. If we Christians forsake Jehovah God, He will abandon us also.

Jehovah God's peace passes our understanding of peace; because mankind does not know or have the peace that our living Jehovah God has. But to us, who are the children of God, He has given us His peace through His son, Jesus Christ, who has believed that God raised Jesus from the dead, who died for mankind's offenses and God raised Him for mankind's justification. Therefore, mankind was justified by faith, and we have peace with God through our lord, Jesus Christ. Jesus gave Mankind his peace who keeps his commandments, but those who serve this world does not have peace. Let not your hearts be troubled or be afraid what man can do to you, but put your trust in the Lord, and He will bring it to pass. Christians must learn how to live happy lives to achieve God's peace. Let us learn to live contented lives in Christ, regardless of our station in this life at any point in our lives journey here on this earth. Let us always look at the things of heaven and not the elements of this earth, and we will have peace.

Jehovah cares for all His creation and mankind should also. God gives names to every star in heaven, and He knows when just one little bird falls dead from the skies and the living does not toil for their food. God sends living waters in rains from the heavens, to water the earth that it may produce foods from the earth to sustain life for all mankind to live. God gave mankind dominion over the animals of the earth and offered them for our food. God gives humanity seasons, and by his word, He controls the weather on earth. Therefore, we must fear our living Jehovah God and keep his commandments because it is

God's good pleasure to give in abundance all good things to those who love and fear Him and keeps his commandments. To all who suffer anxiety in this world, if you seek first the Kingdom of God, which is His church on earth, and follow after God's righteousness, He will care for you and supply all your needs while you live here on earth and when you die, He will give you eternal life in heaven. Fear not, mankind who can kill our bodies but cannot destroy our souls, but let us instead fear Jehovah God who can kill both our bodies and soul in the lake of fire forever and ever without end.

Jehovah God cannot be tempted, nor does He tempt any mankind with an evil of any kind. When mankind is tempted to sin, they are drawn away by their lust and enticed. They are the ones that are weak in the flesh and sin; but Jehovah God is perfect and never sins, even when He punishes mankind for our sins, He is righteous and does not sin.

Jehovah God cannot tell a lie, but mankind is full of myths and idle tales. They also make false reports and swear by them, and there are not very many people on the earth that has integrity today because they cannot be trusted. Jehovah God never tells us a lie so that we can put our trust in Him and He will bring to pass the request of Christian's prayers if they are according to his will and there is nothing wrong with the request we make to him. Yes, let God be true; but every mankind a liar. Trust in God's word, the Holy Bible and not man's word.

Humanity will not mock Jehovah God. Do not deceive yourselves; into thinking that you can do anything, you take pleasure in upon the earth. Because whatsoever we commit in sins, we will receive from God as our punishment for all un-repented of sins. If we sin of the flesh, we will reap the corruption of our flesh. Which will come in the form of sexually transmitted diseases and death? When we sow the seeds of false gods, we will reap destruction and death, and when we plant the seeds of drugs and alcohol, we will reap destruction of our bodies and death. When we sow the seeds of adultery, we will reap divorces, diseases, and broken homes. When we plant the seeds of homosexuality, we will reap the unlawful relationship in God's eyes and a strange union and family, illnesses, and death. When we sow the seeds of hatred, we will receive in the harvest, rioting, strife with others, wantonness, envying of what others have, gluttons, and drowsiness which will bring you down into poverty. Let us sow the seeds in this life on earth to the spirit of Jehovah God, so we can reap eternal life in heaven when we die. Therefore, let us do good unto all Mankind upon the Earth while we live, and especially unto all them that are of the household of faith in God. Every opportunity that we have let us do a good deed for our fellow mankind, keeping us in good grace with God.

Jehovah God loves righteousness, and He hates evil, and He knows where we will live a righteous life or an evil life from our mother's womb. God said by the mouth of the prophets of old time when Rachel has twin boys, one she named Jacob and the other Esau. Jehovah God loved Jacob; because he was righteous all the days of his life, but God hated Esau, because he was evil all the days of his life. Look at the goodness and the severity of our living Jehovah God. Let us examine the severity of His judgments against the wicked, who would not repent of their sins. God threw one-third of the angels out of heaven and put them into Hell;

49

because they wanted to overthrow God. He drowned the world with a flood, except eight souls who were righteous, because they were evil continually and would not repent. He sent fire and brimstone from the heavens and destroyed all the people in Sodom and Gomorrah because they were evil regularly and would not repent. Look, God has said, "Behold, I change not!"

So what will God do with the wicked people of the earth today, who will not repent and serve him? They will be put into hell when they die, and on the last day, God will put them in the lake of fire.

The law of Jehovah God is perfect for converting our soul and His laws are not grievous to bear. The commandment of Jehovah God makes us wise and enlightens our eyes with rejoicing in our hearts. The judgments of God are true and righteous, and there is a high reward to all who keeps them. Christians are to obey the laws of the land; except when man's laws are against the rules of our God. We must abide by God's laws over the requirements of the earth if we want to save our eternal souls.

The ways of Jehovah God are superior to the methods of mankind; Jehovah God is a living god in whom mankind is his offsprings. Therefore, mankind is made in the image and the likeness of Jehovah God. But God has said, "My thoughts are not your thoughts, and My ways are not your ways, for as the heavens are higher than the earth, so are God's ways higher than the means of man."

The key of knowledge to understanding Jehovah God's characteristics is first we must ask ourselves some questions. Why does mankind have the power to reason and animals does not possess these characteristics? Why is it legal to kill animals for our food but it is illegal to kill another human being? Why does mankind have a spirit to know what is right and what is wrong to do but animals don't? Why does mankind have a conscience and animals don't? Well, by now, everyone must understand that mankind was created by someone who possessed the knowledge and power to create us and that was our living Jehovah God. God gave mankind a spirit that will live for eternity in heaven or hell and the Lake of Fire at the end of time. God requires mankind's spirit back when he dies for judgment, but God does not need animals' spirit again, because He never gave them one.

Chapter Seven
God Does Not Pity the Wicked

When the servants of Jehovah God in Israel became wicked, God warned them through His prophet Ezekiel.

"Go and warn the wicked; they shall die in their sins if they do not turn from their wicked ways to save their lives."

But if Ezekiel did not warn the wicked, their blood would be on Ezekiel's hands. However, when Ezekiel warns them of their sins and they do not turn from them, Ezekiel is free from their blood. The same was true for Apostle Paul, when he told the Ephesians Elders that he was free from their blood because he did not shun declaring the whole counsel of God to them. Today, God still required the preachers and teachers of the words of Jehovah God to declare the whole counsel of God unto them or God will require their blood at your hands.

Many of the servants of Jehovah God in Israel fell away from serving Him and went after pagan gods to worship. They defiled the sanctuary where they worshipped these false pagan gods with detestable things, which was an abomination to Jehovah God. God became very angry with them and He passed judgment upon them without pity. God is not the god of the dead in their trespasses and sins; but the god of the living in righteousness.

God does not hear and answer the prayers of the sinners and ungodly, but if anyone is a worshipper of God and does His will, God will hear and answer their prayers. Because the eyes of the Lord are over the righteous and His ears are open to their prayers; but the face of the Lord is against them that do evil.

God did not have pity on the angels that rebelled against God in heaven when God threw them out of heaven down to earth. Then when God sent Jesus Christ to earth, Jesus put Satan and all his angels into hell to await the final judgment. God did not have pity on world of sinners and ungodly people back in the day of Noah. So God caused it to rain on the earth forty days and nights and the floods came and covered the whole earth and drowned all the sinners and ungodly. The people before the flood became vain in their imaginations and their hearts was darkened by their sins. The people gave themselves out to be very wise, but they became fools. God gave them over to a reprobate mind, because their minds was full of uncleanness and they dishonored their own bodies with their homosexual and lesbians acts of unclean sexual acts. They changed the truths of God's words into a lie and worshipped false gods more than they worshipped Jehovah God. They were filled with all manner of sexual immorality and wickedness. They coveted after other people's possessions and they were very envious toward others, showing themselves to be very hateful and malicious toward other People. They were murdering their children as well as other people, moreover, they murdered other people's character with their malignity,

53

setting up innocent people to take a fall for crimes they did not do. They were full of whispering lies against other people and they became backbiters full of deceit. They were haters of God because they rejected his counsels and went about doing what made them feel good and destroying other people. They were inventors of many evil things being very proud and boastful and became disobedient to their parents. They were without understanding and without love for their fellow mankind, without self-control, and they were unmerciful toward other people.

God became disgusted with mankind because their every thought was evil continually and they drifted away from serving the Living God that created them. The people became so wicked that God gave up on them because there was no hope of shining a light on their sins to awaken them and get them to repent and turn back to serving God. Not everyone was physically committing these sins, excluding Noah and his family; however, many of the people were also destroyed in the flood because they supported with pleasure the sins that other people were physically committing and God said there was no difference in them. God did save the righteous people which were Noah and his family.

God destroyed the great cities of Sodom and Gomorrah with raining down from out of heaven's fire and brimstone destroying all the people except Lot and his family, however, Lot's wife disobeyed God's instructions and she looked back at the destruction of those cities and God turned her into a pillar of salt. God did not pity the wicked but had mercy on the righteous.

God will not pity the wicked sinners who will not quit committing sins and the ungodly who have rejected God at the end of time. When God sends Jesus back at the end of time, Jesus will do the same to earth on that day the same thing he had done to Sodom and Gomorrah.

The marvelous thing about my Living Jehovah God is this, when He sent Jonah down to Nineveh to preach God's message to them, God gave those people forty days to repent of their wicked ways, or He would destroy the Great City Nineveh. The people responded from the greatest of them even to the least of them. The King of Nineveh sent, throughout the land, a decree every person and every beast of the land cover themselves with sackcloth and sat in ashes. They repented of their sins and prayed mightily unto God and all the people turned from their evil ways and from committing violence. Now God saw their works, which they had turned from their evil ways, and God repented Himself of the evil He had said He would do to them and God did not destroy them.

Oh, how wonderful is our God, He is full of mercy and forgiveness to everyone who will repent of their wicked ways and turn and serve Him in the Kingdom of God, which is His church here on earth today. Oh, how wonderful is our Living God, today, you can be the most wicked person living on earth, and if you hear the words of God proclaimed and you believe them with all your heart, you confess that Jesus Christ is the son of God and believe in your heart that God raised Him from the dead. You can be baptized for the forgiveness of all your sins and you will be forgiven of every sin you have committed during your lifetime and given the spirit of God to live in your body as your witness.

Every person on the earth knows when they do something evil or something good, this is the power that our living God gave everyone because Adam and Eve ate from the tree of knowledge to know good and evil. Therefore, we do not have any excuses for doing evil, we know better.

God set before all mankind the choice of good and life or evil and death, it is our works that we do in our lives determines where God will give us eternal life or eternal death when our mortal bodies pass from this life. We have the power to determine our eternal destination while we live.

Chapter Eight

We Must Confess and Repent for All Our Sins

God is love and everyone who loves others is born of God and knows God. Those people who do not love one another does not know God; for God is love. God showed His love beyond a shadow of a doubt when us gentiles were lost and without a covenant relationship with Jehovah God. He sent His only begotten son as a sacrifice for our sins. Moreover, the blood that Jesus shed on the cross cleanses our sins when we are baptized for the remission of our sins and God gives us His Spirit to live in our bodies and adds us to the kingdom of God, which is the church.

Once we are born again of God in Baptism and added to the church. If we walk in the light of the truth of the gospels as God is light. We have fellowship with God and He uses the blood of Jesus Christ to cleanse us of all sins when we confess our sins. When Christians pray for forgiveness of our sins, we have Jesus Christ who is our advocate with the Father. Jesus is the propitiation for not only Christians who commit sins but for the sins of the whole world.

How do Christians know they are forgiven of their sins? God commands us not to love in word or tongue, but in doing good deeds and in the truth of the word of God. Hereby. we know we are of the truth and shall assure our hearts before God in our petitions we desire of Him. But if our hearts condemn us, God knows all the Hearts of mankind and knows all things. If our hearts don't condemn us then we have confidence toward God. And whatever we ask of God we receive from Him, because we keep His commandments, and do the things that are pleasing in the sight of God.

If a brother in the Lord Jesus Christ is overtaken in a sin, a Christian that is keeping the commandment of God can go to God in prayer on their behalf and get forgiveness for their sins and restore them back into a relationship with God. All Christians are commanded to bear one another's burdens, so we fulfil the laws of Christ to love one another as he loved us. We must restore a brother or sister with meekness and consider ourselves that we may someday commit a sin and need a righteous brother to pray for us. If a man thinks himself to be something when He is nothing, He deceives Himself; we all mess up sometimes in our lives.

Let God be true and each and every man a liar, because God cannot tell a lie, but mankind can tell lies. There is not even one human who walked on the Earth who never committed a sin, we all have sinned and fell short of the glory of God. But the son of God who became the son of man Jesus Christ was the only person ever to walk upon the earth without any sin!

So let's be as brave and as good as Simon, the Sorcery, who lived in Samaria. When Apostle Philip left Jerusalem and went down to the land of Samaria, he preached Christ unto them, confirming Christ by hearing and seeing the miracles which he did. Philip cast out demons, healed people with palsies and the lame walked. There was great joy in the city and Simon who used sorcery to bewitch people, giving himself out to be a great one. When Simon witnessed the true power from God, he knew he was a fake. But when the people of Samaria believed the things he was preaching concerning the kingdom of God and Jesus Christ, they were baptized into the Kingdom of God. Then Simon himself believed also; and when he was baptized and he continued with Philip seeing the miracles and signs performed by Philip.

When the Church at Jerusalem heard of the great success Philip was having, they sent Apostle Peter and John down to Samaria. Now the members of the church received the gift of the Holy Ghost to live in their bodies as a witness. But when Peter and John laid their hands on the members of the church, they received the power of the Holy Ghost to speak in tongues and prophesied. When Simon, the Sorcery, saw when the apostles laid their hands on them they received the Holy Ghost. Simon wanted to give them money, saying, "Give me also this power, that on whomsoever I lay hands, they may receive the Holy Ghost." Apostle Peter commanded Simon to repent of his wickedness and pray to God to forgive the thoughts of his heart. Simon had thought that the gift of God could be purchased with money; however, all of God's gifts to mankind are given freely without charge. Then Simon asked Apostle Peter to pray to God on his behalf for forgiveness of his sin. This is the gold standard used in the churches of Christians today, meaning this is the commandment of God when Christians commit a sin. First, we pray to God and confess our sins with a broken and contrite heart, even in tears, asking God to forgive us of our sin. Then we request the church to pray for our sin on our behalf, because God will answer the prayers of the righteous who are in good standing with God.

If a brother or sister in the Lord trespass against you, go and tell them their fault between you and them alone; if they repent, you have gained a brother or sister. But if they do not repent then take one or two witnesses with you so every word can be established. If they still will not repent, tell the matter to the elders of the church and let them be unto you as a heathen which is a sinner. Whatsoever is bound by agreement between church members will also be bound in heaven by God and whatsoever is forgiven between churches' members will also be forgiven by God in heaven. Where two or three Christians are gathered together, Jesus Christ is in the midst of them by his Holy Spirit who is a witness of all the works of Christians. Therefore, whatsoever is bound between Christians on earth will be bound by God in heaven.

This same principle should be used when Christians owe a debt and have no intentions of repaying. God commands us not to owe anyone anything; but to love one another, for this is our obligation. God commands us Christians to forgive one another of our trespasses against one another or He will not forgive us our trespasses when we mess up.

Christians who are made stewards over other people's goods, such as their estates, businesses, institutions, government offices, and God requires us to be good stewards over their affairs. If we embezzle part of their wealth, then we must make restitution.

Christians must never commit character assignation by making false allegation's detrimental to the character of others. Do not gossip or whisper secrets against other people because this is a sin. We can use the same principle as Simon, the Sorcery, used to get forgiveness of his sin.

Christians must not commit the willful sin of omission of forsaking going to church to worship God. Christians must follow the same formula as Simon, the Sorcery, to get forgiveness. You must return back to the congregation and repent before them and have the church to pray on your behalf. When we forsake God He will forsake us. Do not forsake assembling every Sunday with the brethren at the church. This is a commandment from God.

Christians must never commit the sin of holding the truth of God in unrighteousness. We are without excuse; we have the words of God in the Bible. Do not change the words of God written in the Holy Bible into a lie, moreover, do not debate the Holy Bible for this is a sin. We can reason among ourselves of things written in the Scriptures, but God's words rule. Preachers, elders, and teachers of God's word do not commit this sin. If you do, we must use the same rule as Simon, the Sorcery, used when sinning before the church.

Christians must not support by taking pleasure in the Sinners and Ungodly people who commit sins. God destroyed those people right along with the people who actually done the crimes by the flood.

Now I testify to you and before everyone in heaven and on Earth, of the great mercy and forgiveness of my beloved God and Father in heaven. When God sent my guardian angel from heaven in 2011 to rebuke and chastise me for making false allegations in my prayers to God and for my sins. All of these things are written in detail in my book called *My Guardian Angel Visits* by Jerry Campbell and published by West Bow Press. You can order on my web site: www.thelakeoffireisrealandhereonearth.com

The angel told me when I talked to him, I was talking to God and when I said, "You are not god," he replied, "No, Jerry, but when you talk to me, God hears you and He tells me what to say to you."

So I communicated with God in heaven for about thirty minutes. God knew my entire life, even the things that were done in secret. Moreover, when I confessed and repented with tears my sins, God forgave me for them, He also forgave me of a sin that I worried about from time to time because I didn't know how to get rid of the sin and a sin that God doesn't think that I knew was a sin. This is how great God's love and mercy is.

Chapter Nine

God Manifested Himself Through His Son, Jesus Christ

In the Old Testament, God spoke to Mankind through his prophets, but in the New Testament, God spoke to Mankind through His son, Jesus Christ. God was manifested in the flesh by His son, Jesus Christ; therefore, the works of Christ are the works of his Father God. Moreover, all the great qualities of Jesus Christ written in the New Testament also show the great qualities of Jehovah God to Mankind.

Here are some of the greatest from Jehovah God that He bestowed upon mankind through, His son Jesus Christ.

Grace came to all mankind through Jesus Christ. During the time of the Old Testament, God punished many sins with stoning to death immediately, but when Jesus came to Earth God extended grace for our sins through repentance of those sins. Also when people today hear and believe the word of God, if they confess the Lord Jesus with their mouth and believe in their heart that God raised Him from the dead, they shall be saved. Therefore, mankind is saved by grace, because every sin and transgression they ever committed during their lifetime is all forgiven at baptism. However, mankind is judged by our faith and works; thereby, we are saved or lost by our faith and works.

Christians today can fall from the grace that Jesus gave us in our salvation. Christ has become of no effect to the Christian who justifies themselves by the Old Testament laws. We have fallen from Grace. Christians who look into the perfect law of liberty and continues therein, and be not a forgetful hearer but a doer of the work, this Christian will be greatly blessed in their deeds. So Christians must speak and do according to the law of liberty because we will be judged by this law.

Before God sent Jesus Christ to earth, we gentiles were without a covenant relationship with Jehovah God. Therefore, the greatest gift that God gave us gentiles through Jesus Christ was listed in Jesus' mission statement. When Jesus began his ministry, he went into the Synagogue at Nazareth, where he was brought up and he read to the people. The spirit of the Lord is upon me because he hath anointed me to preach the gospel to the poor; he hath anointed me to heal the brokenhearted, to preach deliverance to the captives, and recover the sight of the blind, and set at liberty them that are bruised. And preach the acceptable year of the Lord.

Wow! What a great God is Jehovah God? We gentiles were held captive by the power of Satan because our forefathers rejected serving Jehovah God. But Jesus Christ became our savior when he turned us gentiles from the power of darkness of sins to the light of the world Jesus Christ who gave us the truth from God. Jesus Christ set us gentiles free from the power of Satan who held us captive to sin and death. Jesus Christ gave us gentiles the light of the gospels and eternal life in heaven. Thank God Almighty, we gentiles are free from Satan.

Look at the compassion of God which was manifested by Jesus Christ: God was not willing the world should continue without first including us gentiles in a covenant relationship with Him. God was not satisfied with the first covenant whereby mankind's sins was rolled back for one year only by using the blood of bulls and goats. God uses the blood of His son, Jesus Christ, that He shed on the Cross to forgive mankind's sins forever, never to remember again.

Look at how God is full of meekness and lowly which was manifested by Jesus Christ: God lived in the body of Jesus Christ while He was here on earth by his holy spirit which is the power of God. Look into the Holy Bible and witness the acts of Jesus Christ, there was never any person ever walk upon this earth that is worthy of being good as Jesus Christ. Jesus gave us gifts that is priceless and cannot be purchased with this world's money or goods. The gift of salvation of our souls, the gift of grace and truth, repent and get forgiveness of our sins, baptism by water and all our sins are forgiven forever wherefore we committed before baptism. Jesus gave us the Kingdom of God which is His church to worship God on Sunday; Jesus gave us the Holy Spirit of God and Christ to live in all obedient Christian's bodies to help Christians with our lives on earth.

Look at the goodness of God which was manifested by Jesus Christ on earth.

Consider all the people Jesus healed from blindness, cast out demons, healed the deft and dumb, cured the insane mind, and healed the lame and halt. Jesus raised the dead, healed the paralytic, and healed the lepers, which is a flesh-eating disease called leprosy. And many other miraculous things Jesus performed before the eyes of thousands of witnesses. Jesus went about the earth doing good during his three year ministry fulfilling his mission from God.

When the rich, young ruler came to Jesus and asked, "Good Master, what good thing can I do to inherit eternal life?"

Jesus said, "Why call me 'good'? There is none good except God."

Jesus told us, "Truly, truly, I tell you, the son can do nothing of himself, but what he sees the father do: for whatsoever he does, these things the son does also. Because the father loves the son, and shows him all things he does."

O what power did God give His son, Jesus Christ, on earth, Jesus walked on water, feed five thousand people with three fish and two loaves of bread, because God opened the windows of heaven and poured baskets full of fish and bread from heaven. Jesus raised Lazarus from the dead and he was dead for four days and his body was decaying; but when Lazarus walked out of the grave, he was completely whole. God gave Jesus the power of resurrection and over life of mankind.

O what power did God bestow upon Jesus Christ for accomplishing God's mission to earth for him! God gave Jesus power over all the earth and heaven, except power over God. Jesus was given the power to judge all mankind, giving him the power of eternal life in heaven or eternal death in hell. And at his coming for the final judgment day, Jesus will give mankind eternal life or eternal death in the Lake of Fire which will be on this present earth.

O what power did God give Jesus Christ! God gave Jesus power over the Holy Ghost and the holy angels. The Holy Spirit is a witness for Jesus and God of everything that all mankind does whether we do evil or good and they know the very thought of our minds. The Holy Spirit is everywhere on earth at the same time and he reports all things whatsoever he witnessed to Jesus Christ in heaven for our judgment. The Holy Spirit sees all things, knows all things, and hears all things, and witnesses all things on the earth today.

The wisdom of God was manifested to the world through Jesus Christ. When Jesus began his ministry, mankind did not know about hell or paradise and heaven. Jesus showed mankind the way to get to heaven and the way to hell. We must follow in the footprints of Jesus as taught and recorded in the Holy Bible for the salvation of our souls. God taught mankind the new laws of God through Jesus Christ; moreover, the words that Jesus spoke to us God told Jesus what to say. God taught us about the family and the duties of the father, mother, and children. God taught us about adultery and divorce and the laws governing sexual immorality.

Once God taught us through Jesus the new plan of salvation, Jesus taught us by example how to do good work in the kingdom of God to be judged fit for the Kingdom of Heaven. Jesus taught us we are saved by grace but we are judged by our faith and our works. Jesus taught before his death on the cross people were judged by the Old Testament Laws, and after his death, people will be judged by the New Testament Laws. Jesus taught us about the book of life in heaven and how people are written in the book of life and taken out of the book of life.

Moreover, God taught us through Jesus Christ how to enter into the church he purchased with his bloodshed on the Cross. First Jesus taught us to enter into the church through the straight and narrow way; thereby, we must follow His plan to be saved. First, you must hear the word of God preached and this will give you faith in God. Second, you must believe the word of God in order to receive anything from God; thereby, you must confess Jesus before the congregation openly and believe in your heart God raised Jesus from the dead you shall be saved. Thereby, you must be baptized in water for the remission of your sins and God will give you the gift of His Holy Spirit to live in your body and He will be your witness to Jesus Christ who will judge all mankind.

Well, this is how wonderful and valuable Jehovah God has been to me. If I owned the entire world and everything in the world and I gave it all to God, it would not repay my debt I owe Him. I love God and believe in God more than anyone in heaven and anyone on earth.

Chapter Ten

God Is Omnipresent, Being Everywhere at the Same Time

Jehovah God has known me from my mother's womb, and He gave me my name before I was born. He knows what I will do from my mother's womb until I die, He knows the very thoughts and intents of my heart from heaven. Jehovah God knows all the paths of my life, and He knows every word that my tongue will ever speak. My Christian mother taught me the Holy Scriptures from my youth, and she taught me to fear God as she read everything in the Holy Scriptures about hell and the Lake of Fire. When Mother showed me the awesome power and love that God has for poor people, this set my heart on fire to know all the knowledge I could learn about Him. When I was a young man, I made my bed, living on the wild side of this life; but when I started to read the Holy Bible by myself, God would make my heart beat faster, and I could feel the blood rushing through my body when I read the new testament words written in red, which are the words that Jehovah God gave Jesus Christ to teach mankind. These words are "spirit" and "life."

O! Dear Jehovah God, where can I go from your Holy Spirit and where could I flee from your presence? You know me better than I know me, you know every sin that I have ever committed, even the sins that I have done in secret and under cover of darkness. You formed me in my mother's womb, and you wove me, I will praise you because you have made me wonderfully; marvelous are all your works from the beginning until the end. Your eyes, O God, have seen everything that I have ever done from my birth to this day, Oh, how I cherish your great love for me. You, O God, have given me more excellent and perfect gifts than I can count and I thank you and love you for every one of them. You have saved my life from death more than once in my lifetime. Once when I was sick unto death, you heard and answered my crying prayers to you, and you answered them from heaven, sending my guardian angel to heal me and save me. You, O my God, you keep me from wild boar in the mountains, from a car wreck that was a total loss of the car and there was not a hair on my head injured. You saved me from a cold-blooded killer who robbed my store, from killing me as he said he would. You, O God, saved me from a deadly rattlesnake that was ready to strike me with his fatal poison bite when I was a young boy in the mountains in Eastern Kentucky. Many other times, my beloved heavenly Father, you have shown me your kind and loving hand from heaven, supplying me with all my needs upon this earth.

The secret to Jehovah God having the ability to be in all places at the same time is this, God is a spirit, and he has a spirit called the Holy Ghost. The Holy Ghost is the source of power for Jehovah and Jesus Christ. I refer to the Holy

Ghost as their workhorse; because God and Christ give him commands and he does them. The Holy Ghost is the third person in the God Head and He assisted God in the Creation. He also raised Jesus from the dead, and if Christians die with the Holy Ghost living in their bodies, He will raise them from the dead at the last day when Jesus Christ gives the Command. The Holy Ghost relays all the Christian's prayers to Jehovah God, whether vocal or silent prayers, God hears them and answers them. The Holy Ghost will bear witness to Jehovah God in heaven of every person that has ever lived upon the Earth. He will justify or condemn everyone, including the Christians, sinners, and the ungodly. No one can flee from the power of the Holy Ghost, and He will be on earth until the end of time.

The Holy Ghost is the Spirit of Jehovah God and Jesus Christ; because there is just one God, one Lord, and one Spirit. Now we know how Jesus does it when he declared, where there are two or three gathered in my name there I am in the midst of them! Indeed He is there and He knows every word and every thought that we say or think by His Spirit! There three witnesses that bear a record of everyone that ever lived on Earth. That is Jehovah God, Jesus Christ, and the Holy Ghost, and these three are one and these three that bears witness upon the earth, that is the Holy Spirit, the water baptism, and Jesus' bloodshed on the Cross and these three agree in one! There are no other living gods, no other living witnesses, in heaven or on earth, except these three!

Now I testify before these three witnesses in heaven and on earth, that Jehovah God sent my guardian angel from heaven to visit me and I communicated with Jehovah God and Jesus Christ in heaven through their Holy Angel, they sent to rebuke and chastise me for my sins. The angel said when I spoke to him that God hears me and tells him what to say to me, this is how I talked with God and Christ in heaven. Every word of this visit was recorded in my book called *My Guardian Angel Visits* published by West Bow Press.

Oh, let me give thanks to my living merciful God when I repented of my sins of making a false accusation against God in my silent prayer and having unlawful women in my life. When I repented with a broken heart with tears of sorrow, my God and Father in heaven. He had mercy upon my soul and forgave me of my sins. And then He showed me more mercy abundantly by forgiving me also of two sins that I had committed, one I worried about from time to time and didn't know how to get rid of that sin and one sin I determined that I didn't realize a sin. Since I repent with bitter tears the two sins aforementioned, Jehovah God had grace and mercy and forgave me for every crime that I had ever, and He wrote my name back into the Book of Life in heaven. Thank you, Jehovah God, for your great mercy to me, Your mercy endures forever, and I will always have mercy for others.

Oh, let me give praises to my living Jehovah God, for whatever He pleases, He does in heaven or earth. He is the only God, the gods of others are idols, they are dead men, or they are gods of silver or gold. Having mouths, but they do not speak, having eyes, but they do not see, having ears, but they do not hear, they have no breath in their mouths! Those who worship them are like them. Bless my Heavenly Father and God who has a mouth to speak with, eyes to see with, ears to hear with, and a heart to show goodness and mercy.

Christians that have been born again in water baptism all receive the gift of the Holy Ghost to live in our bodies as our witness to God and Christ in heaven. The Holy Ghost gives us Christians the wisdom to understand the Scriptures. The Holy Bible is the work of the Holy Ghost, whereas He spoke through the prophets and the holy men of old time to deliver the words of Jehovah God to them and He spoke through the apostles to provide the words that God delivered through Jesus Christ to the apostles. The Holy Ghost is given to the obedient Christians and they are not to resist, quench, or grieve the Holy Ghost. The Holy Ghost was sent down from heaven to convict the sinners and the ungodly of the world in judgment, but He will justify the Christians. The Holy Ghost teaches us Christians, and He leads us in the paths of righteousness, He gives us the knowledge to understand the Holy Scriptures.

The Holy Ghost is the spirit of eternal life and He gives us Christians comfort, hope, joy, and truth. The Holy Ghost regenerates all believers that are born again of God in baptism. The world of sinners and ungodly cannot receive the Holy Ghost, He will not live in their bodies, but live in the obedient Christian body. Praise Jehovah God for the Gift of his Holy Ghost, for He is the power of God and Christ. Thank you, Jehovah God, for your spirit.

The unforgivable sin that mankind can commit is the blasphemy against the Holy Ghost, there is never forgiveness in this world or the world to come. The ungodly who have committed blasphemy against God, done so ignorantly and If they later in their life have a change of heart and truly follow the plan of salvation, God will forgive them at their Baptism. The great apostle Paul was a prime example of this, and He was a blasphemer against the Holy Ghost before Jesus converted him to Christianity, but it is the Christians who can sin blasphemy against the Holy Ghost today. How can Christians commit this sin today after we have come to God and been partakers of God's benefit's and then we turn away from serving God by quit going to church and worshipping God? And then when trouble sets in on our lives when we begin to talk evil against God, denying Him, and then we have committed blasphemy against God Holy Spirit.

The key to knowledge to understanding how Jehovah God can be in all places at the same time is to know everything in the scriptures about the Holy Ghost. Humanity has a spirit that God gave every one of us, He requires back upon the death of our bodies. Our soul is like the Holy Ghost in that our soul is invisible and it departs out of our bodies upon the end of our bodies. The Holy Ghost is the spirit of God and Christ, and He is the third person in the Godhead. God is a spirit, Jesus Christ is a spirit, the Holy Ghost is a spirit, the angels in heaven are spirits, and all mankind has a spirit living in us. All mankind who are saved will be equal to the angels residing in the New Heaven and New Earth. The key to knowledge to understanding how God can be omnipresent, being in all places at all times is accepting the critical work of the Holy Ghost of God.

Chapter Eleven

God Is Omnipotent, Having Unlimited Powers and Authority

Jehovah God created everything in heaven and everything on earth; He created Jesus and all the angels in heaven, He created all the planets and stars and named them one by one. After some six hundred billion years later, God decided to make the earth inhabited by mankind and animals; at that time the earth was covered entirely with water and was void of any living thing upon the planet. The earth's form today was made by our Living Creator, whose name is the Almighty Jehovah God. I testify that I have witnessed the power of the Almighty God first hand, whereas He has heard my prayers and answered them, sending my guardian angel from heaven to heal me and show me in a vision the Lake of Fire that will come upon the earth at the last day. And again the Almighty God sent my guardian angel to visit me, after God put me in a trance, showing me the night that I made a vow to him for healing me, saving me from certain death. I testify that I talked with Jehovah God and Jesus Christ in heaven through the Holy Angel that God sent to rebuke me of my sin's that were un-repented of and not living up to my vow. These are all written in the title of my books The Lake of Fire Is Real and Here on Earth and My Guardian Angel visits by Jerry Campbell.

Jesus declared the power of his father Jehovah God when He told his disciples that is was easier for a camel to go through the eye of a needle, that for a rich man to enter into the Kingdom of Heaven. Then his disciples asked Jesus, who then can be saved? Jesus declared that with men this is impossible, but with God, all things are possible. Everything that is in heaven and on the earth belongs to Jehovah God, for God owns everything and everyone. God has the power to take away everything that mankind holds, and He can give whatever He wants to mankind. Therefore, let us be wise and not provoke God, because God has the power to destroy both our bodies and our soul in hell and on the last day in the Lake of Fire for eternity. Let us read the Holy Scriptures and be endued with knowledge of God, for He is much to be feared and held in reverence by all the people of the earth and in heaven.

Jehovah God overrules human plans because God knows the future of everyone that lives on earth. God gives us a perfect example of Gods servant Jacob who lived in the land of Canaan. God caused Joseph to dream dreams that signified the future, but his family failed to interpret the dreams. Joseph was the youngest of Jacob's ten sons and he loved him more because Joseph was the son in his old age. Joseph brothers hated him because Joseph dreamed he was in the field sheaving grain and his sheave stood upright, and His Brothers sheaves bowed down to his sheave. Then he imagined that the sun, and the moon, and eleven stars bowed down to him. There came a day when Joseph brothers went to feed the flocks and had not returned and Jacob was worried about them, and He sent Joseph the youngest brother to find them and bring him back a report. Now when His brothers looked and saw Joseph coming afar off they plotted to kill him, here comes the dreamer wearing the coat of many colors that his mother made for him, which Joseph loved the coat. Then Reuben, the eldest brother said, "Let us not kill him, nor harm him, but throw him in the empty pit. And here comes a band of Ishmaelites going down to Egypt to sell their products," when Joseph's brother, Judah, saw them coming, He talked his brothers into selling Joseph, so they took Joseph down to Egypt and traded him to Potiphar who was an officer in pharaoh army.

It came to pass while God was blessing Potiphar's house for Joseph's sake that His wife had eyes for Him and when Joseph rejected her many times, she accused him of coming on to her and asking her for sex. And Potiphar had Joseph put into prison, And God showed Joseph Mercy and gave him favor in the eyes of the warden. And the warden of the prison put Joseph in charge of all the prisoners, and whatever Joseph did, God made it to prosper.

It came to pass that pharaoh had two dreams that trouble him, and he called together all his magicians and wise men to interpret the dreams and they could not. Then pharaoh was told by the butler that was in the prisoner with Joseph how Joseph had interpreted his dream and it came to pass. So pharaoh sent for joseph to go to him and explain his dreams. Jehovah God had warned pharaoh in his dreams what he was going to bring to pass in all the countries. Jehovah God would give every nation seven years of plenty, and after that, He would give them seven years of famine. Since Joseph was full of the Spirit of God is full of wisdom above all the other interpreters, pharaoh made him overseer over the whole Land of Egypt, giving Joseph power over everyone in the land, except pharaoh only. Joseph went all over Egypt during the seven years of plenty. He built food storages all over Egypt during the seven years of plenty so that they could live off the foods during the seven years of famine. After seven years of famine, it would deplete all the reserves of food.

Then it came to pass in the land of Canaan, and the famine was so bad where Joseph's family lived that Jacob sent his sons down to Egypt to buy food. When the brothers came before their brother, Joseph, they did not recognize him; but Joseph recognized them. Joseph sold them the food, but He put their money for the feedback into their sacks. When they were going back home to Canaan, Joseph sent his servants to find them and bring them back to Egypt. When his brothers came before his face, Joseph could not restrain himself when he looked at his brother's, and he went into a private room and wept aloud. Then Joseph came before his brothers and said, "I am Joseph, does my father still live?"

His brothers could not answer him for they were dismayed in his presence. Then Joseph said to his brothers, "Please, come near to me, I am Joseph, your brother, whom you sold into Egypt. But do not be grieved or angry with yourselves because you sold me here; for God sent me before you to preserve life. For these two years, famine has been in the land, and we still have five more years to go, in which there will be no harvesting. And it was Jehovah God who sent me before you to preserve a posterity for you in the earth and save your lives by a great deliverance. So it was not you who sent me here, but God, and He made me a father to pharaoh, and the lord of all His house, and a ruler throughout all the land of Egypt."

Jehovah God can overrule human designs, and He sets up the plans for his servants that serve, and love him when they keep his commandments. Joseph and his father, Jacob, chosen and called Jehovah God to help him. Jehovah God also overrules the human designs of the sinner and ungodly who do not serve him. There was a certain rich man who planted his crops, and they brought forth such a great harvest, that the rich man said to himself. What shall I do with all this harvest, I know what I will do, I will tear down all my small barns and build bigger barns to store all my harvest. And I will say to my soul, and you have many goods stored up, let's take it easy for the rest of our lives and be merry. Jehovah God was seeing how the rich man didn't want to help the sick and starving People with any food, So God said, "You fool, tonight I will require your soul and then who will all these things belong?"

Let us always be humble and kind to all people upon the earth, never let our possessions make us think that we are something when we are nothing in God's eyes when we have plenty and will not help our fellow mankind when we see them in need of food, water, or clothing.

What a mighty awesome power God had shown to mankind when He sent Jesus from heaven to earth. Jesus being a grown spirit in heaven, but was born to a virgin named Mary as a baby boy and God fashioned Jesus after earthly boys. Mary asked the Angel Gabriel, "How can these things be since I know not a man?"

Gabriel told Mary that God's Holy Spirit would come upon her and He would overshadow her. Therefore, the holy one that is born will be called the son of God. God brought Jesus from heaven when He was a grown spirit man and prepared a human body for him in the womb of a virgin woman, being born on earth as a baby boy. No one else in heaven or on earth has the power to accomplish such a mighty task as this, except Jehovah God.

Jehovah God has put down the mighty from their thrones and exalted the lowly. God sets up nations, and He takes down nations. God has mercy on them that fear him, God scatters the proud in heart with their evil imaginations. He fills the hungry with good things and sends the rich away empty. Jehovah God is like a father taking care of his children, to all nations that fear Him and keeps his commandments. But the evil nations Jehovah God is far from them, and his face is against them that He will not hear their prayers; their sins have separated them from Jehovah God.

The nations that are set up by Jehovah God are the ones that fear him and keeps his commandments. Every soul is to be subject to the governing authorities of those nations, because there is no authority except it be from God. Therefore, whosoever resists the power resists the ordinance of God, and those who oppose will bring the judgment of God upon themselves. People who obey the laws have no fear of the authorities, but those who do evil should be afraid of the authorities because they are God's ministers, an avenger to execute punishment on them that practices evildoing.

The key to knowledge of understanding the almighty power of our living Jehovah God is this. First, you must believe that there is a living God and you must have a fear of Him; for this is the beginning of our knowledge about God. Must we ask ourselves these questions? And reason in our hearts the answer to them. Where did the sun, moon, all planets, and stars come? Where did the animals of the land, air, and sea come? Why is it so that only humans and animals can have life on the planet earth, but they cannot live on any other planet in the solar system? Why is earth the only planet suited for mankind to live therein? Where did we human beings come from at the beginning of time? Well, there is not any human being that ever lived in the past, present, or in the future with the knowledge to answer these questions! That is because Jehovah God has established the earth as the boundaries of mankind dwelling and we cannot exceed God's power or plan.

Chapter Twelve

God Maintains the Nature
of the Earth

After Jehovah God created mankind, He never left them alone to fend for themselves; moreover, God created the entire nature of the earth and He never left mankind alone to take care of all His creation. God gave us seasons; spring, summer, fall, and winter, and during the past six billion years the earth has existed the temperature of the earth has never become two percent colder or hotter. God made the earth to last until the end of earth time as we know it.

God is keeping this earth in store for the end of time, but the beginning of eternity where there is no days or nights, no months or years, no seasons. But on that day the Lord will come and the heavens shall pass away with a great noise, and all the elements of the earth will melt with a fervent heat, and the earth also and all the things of the earth will all be burned up. At this time all the stars, moon, sun, and all the planets in the heavens shall be dissolved, and the elements shall melt with a fervent heat as they pass away.

God is the maker and giver of all things; therefore, He owns everything. God made mankind and our spirits that will live forever and ever in heaven or the Lake of Fire here on this earth, according to the life each and every one of us decide to live here on earth.

The country of Israel in the city of Jerusalem during King David's reign, God blessed greatly. God numbers all the Stars and gives them names; He has great power and understanding. God lifts up the meek and cast down the wicked people of the earth. God gives the birds and animals their food, and He takes pleasure in the people who fear Him and hope in his mercy. God blessed Israel with peace in their borders and fills them with the finest wheat. God covers the heavens with clouds and gives the earth its rain; He has strengthened the bars of the gates and blessed the children within your gates. God gives snow like wool, and frost like ashes, and ice like morsels. Then God sends out his word and melts them, He sends out His commandments upon the earth and they are quick and powerful. Blessed is the nation whose God is Jehovah who turns from their vanities of their sin and serve the living God who made heaven and earth and sea, and all things that are therein. In times past, God suffered nations to walk in their own ways. However, the Jewish people chose to serve him, and they are his witness of God who did well and gave them rain from heaven and fruitful seasons, filling their hearts with food and gladness. God does all these things and more for all the Christians who obey his commandments in the New Testament.

Jesus has power over the forces of nature like God. One day Jesus sent his disciples to the other side of the sea to Bethsaida while He went up into the mountains to pray. When the evening came, Jesus looked out to sea and saw the disciples in a bad storm struggling to row the ship. Jesus went to them walking upon the sea, and when they saw him they cried out with fear, saying is it a spirit, but immediately Jesus spoke to them, saying, "Be of good cheer, it is I, be not afraid."

And Peter said, "Lord, if it be you; bid me come to you on the water."

Jesus said, "Come," but when Peter got down out of the ship and began walking on the water, he saw the boisterous winds and he became afraid and began to sink, begging the Lord to save him. Immediately, Jesus stretched out his hand and caught Peter and said, "O, you of little faith, why did you doubt?"

When they came and got back into the ship the wind ceased and the disciples were amazed and came and worshipped Jesus. God and Jesus Christ have power over the forces of nature on earth.

When Apostle Paul was sailing on a ship to Rome to testify of the Lord Jesus, there arose a mighty storm in the sea. The storm was so bad that all the people of the ship lost all hope of being saved. After a long time, Paul stood in the midst of the ship and said, "You should have listened to me and not left Crete only to gain this harm and loss. And now I exhort you to be of good cheer: for there shall be no loss of any man's life, except the loss of the ship. For there stood by me, this night, the angel from God of whom I serve. The angel told me to fear not Paul: you must be brought before Cesar and God has given you all them that sail with you. Wherefore be of good cheer, for I believe God that it shall be just as the angel told me. Howbeit, we must be cast upon a certain island which was Melita."

When God created the heavens and the earth and everything in them, God made them to last forever or to meet His purpose. Consider us humans; we could live forever on this earth if it was God's purpose. Because God put the seed to reproduce another human in the man and when He comes together with his wife, she conceives this seed bringing forth another human into the world. Moreover, God put the seed to reproduce another after its own kind in every male species on the earth. Likewise, when they come together the female of the species reproduces another after its own kind, and this is so with every living creature on the earth.

God used the same "Law of Nature" when He created all the trees, grass, herbs, and vegetables, and flowers of the earth. God put the seed within every one of these to reproduce again after its own kind on the earth. Moreover, God put the same kind of blood in every race of mankind upon the earth, but He put a different kind of blood in the entire animals. How much does God love his creation? Well, God knows when just one tiny sparrow bird falls dead out of the skies. God loves His creation and He provides all their needs for survival until the Judgment Day.

Do not be deceived God is not mocked; God did not spare the angels that sinned in heaven, but He threw them in hell to await the final judgment. God did not spare Sodom and Gomorrah but destroyed them with fire and brimstone. God did not spare the people on the other side of the flood who were evil continually; but destroyed all but eight souls with a great flood. God will not do for us what He did not do for all these people before us. God outlines in the Holy Bible His plans for mankind at the end of earth time. Be not deceived this day will come when you least expect it; if you do not believe God.

Jehovah God maintains the nature of all the Earth; he made the sun and moon to be a perpetual source to govern night and day. Moreover, they give us our seasons, days, months, and years. They also regulate our temperature of the earth whereas the earth has never become over two degrees hotter or colder in any given period of time.

Chapter Thirteen

God Is Omniscience, Knowing the Past, Present, and Future

I can testify to you that I know this to be right first hand. When Jehovah God sent my guardian angel to visit me in 2011, He rebuked me for making a false claim against God in my prayers to Him. Also, God chastised me for not living up to my vows that I made to Him in 1950 when I was sick unto certain death. I was committing the sin of having unlawful women in my relationships, other than my lawful wife that He gave me. When I repented of these sins in bitter tears before God, He forgave me of the sins that I repented of and also showed me great mercy. And forgave me of a crime that I committed in 1986 and did not know how to correct the sin, even He forgave me of a sin that I committed that I did not realize it was a sin to do. Then Jehovah God wrote my name back into the Book of Life in heaven.

Jehovah God knows all things that are in the past, present, and the future; because He is the beginning of all things and the father of all things in heavens and on earth. God knows the past because He has lived history; He is from everlasting to everlasting. When I was standing before

God's holy angel who was my guardian angel, God knew my entire past, He knew my thoughts before I spoke them, and He knew my future. Because God promised me that when I died, I would go to heaven.

Jehovah God has the power of infinity and is eternal, He always was, and is now, and will no Limit or End to His power and rule. God gave names to all the stars, And knows when one sparrow falls dead out of the sky, God has every hair on mankind's head all numbered and knows when every one of us will die because He has determined our pre-appointed time here on earth. God has already pre-appointed a day in which He will judge the world by His son, Jesus Christ. Jehovah God only knows when this day will come.

The depth of Jehovah God's riches in His wisdom and knowledge are unsearchable by mankind, and His judgments and ways are past mankind finding out. There is no one in heaven or on earth that knows the mind of Jehovah God, and no one has ever been a counsellor to Jehovah God. All things in heaven and on earth, all things that are made by Him, through Him, and for Him. All the treasures of wisdom and knowledge are in Jehovah God, and He tells it all to mankind on a need to know basis.

Jehovah God can see us humans here on earth, all the way from heaven. The Lord Jesus once said, "As I see and hear, I judge and this would be from heaven."

I testify unto you that when Jehovah God sent His holy angel, which was my guardian angel from heaven, to chastise me for my sins. The angel told me that God loved to hear me tell the story of what God has done for me in 1950. All these things are written in my two books that I wrote and published by West Bow Press, the titles, *The Lake of Fire Is Real and Here on Earth* and *My Guardian Angel Visits* by author Jerry Campbell. Recorded in these two books are my testimonies how that Jehovah God saw, heard, and knew my entire life here on earth and He never left heaven.

Jehovah God's presence is everywhere at the same time, some of the prophets of old time, such as Jonah tried to flee from the presence of Jehovah God; but He could not. The Prophet-King David asked God, "Where can I go or where can I flee from your Holy Spirit? If my soul ascends up to heaven, you are there; if my soul descends to hell, you are there, also."

Jesus Christ declared in the Gospels, "When I go back to heaven, I will send you the Holy Spirit and He will be with you, and He will be a witness to every act of righteous of mankind and He will be a witness to every sin of mankind, and He will testify of these acts of mankind in their judgment. When the Holy Spirit comes, He also will bring all things to your memory, whatsoever I have taught you. And He will show you of things to come, and He will glorify me, and whatsoever I tell Him, He will explain it to you. All things that Jehovah God has are mine also, so the spirit of God is also my spirit."

When Rebekah, who was Isaac's wife, was pregnant with twins, they wrestled in her womb. This troubled Rebekah, so she went to Jehovah God in prayers and asked God what this meant. God told Rebekah, "Two nations are in your womb, two peoples shall be separated from your body; one people shall be stronger than the other, and the older shall serve the younger."

So the first one of the twins to be born was Esau, He was red and hairy all over his body, and the younger twin born was Jacob, he was a mild-mannered man, and lived in tents. One day, Jacob cooked his mother a stew and Esau came in from the hunting fields, whereas he was a skilled hunter. And as they were eating, Esau was very hungry and asked Jacob to give him some of red stew and Jacob said sell me your birthright for the stew. Esau was so hungry that he was about to die, so he sold Jacob his birthright. The heritage in those days gave one the legal rights to inherit the estates of their fathers, so this is how the firstborn, Esau, was to serve the younger born Jacob. Esau did evil all the days of his life and Jacob did righteous all the days of his life. So God loved Jacob and He hated Esau, because God hates the evil that mankind does.

The key to knowledge to understanding how Jehovah God can have the power to know everything in the past and everything in the present and everything in the future. Is on this wise mankind must trace his genealogy back to Jehovah God, for He must realize that we came from God in our beginning. We must recognize that our God is a living God and we are created in his image and likeness, with all the characteristics that our living God possesses. Humankind must realize that all things are possible for God to accomplish, but mankind is limited in our powers. We cannot remember everything in the past of our lives, we forget many things, But God never forgets anything. And in the present, all we know is what we see, hear, and feel at present; but God knows what everyone in the whole world and heaven is doing at all times of the day or night. All mankind knows about the future for sure, is we will all someday die; but God knows what every one of us will do, all the days of our lives on earth, but it will be our choice of what we do. We are the master of our final destination in eternity, if we do good things on earth our home will be in heaven; but if we do evil things here on earth, our eternal home will be in hell and at the end of time, The Lake of Fire.

The mystery to understanding how Jehovah God does this impressive task with hundred percent precision hundred percent of all the times. The mystery rests in the works of the Holy Spirit of God here on earth in the birth, life, and death, and resurrection of Jesus Christ. The mystery rests in the fact that the Holy Spirit of God gave Moses and the prophets the old Scriptures from God and He gave Jesus and His apostles the New Testament from the mouth of Jehovah God. So all the scriptures are the oracles of Jehovah God, and they are the work of the Holy Spirit of God. The Holy Spirit of God and Christ is a critical member of the Godhead; because He is their witness here on Earth. This is why God made the sin of blasphemy against the Holy Ghost, the crime that will never be forgiven in this world or the world to come. Christians are commanded not to grieve, quench, or resist the Holy Ghost.

Jehovah God knows every person born on earth while they are in their mother's womb and He gives us our names before we are born. God numbers every step that we will take upon the earth before we die and He counts every hair on our head. Before we are born, God appoints unto us a day that we will die and Judged. God has appointed the bounds of mankind's home, and it is the earth, we cannot live beyond these bounds of our habitation. God knows our lives before we are born, whether we will live a good life and serve him, or we will live an evil life and be lost; but it is our choice to make, but He knows what we will choose before we choose. God knows every thought and every word that we speak from our birth until our death by the work of his Holy Spirit on earth.

The mystery of the Holy Ghost is on this wise; He is invisible, just like the ghost of all mankind, whereas when we die, we give up our ghost and it is required back to Jehovah God. The Holy Ghost is the source of the power of God and Christ, and He is a member of the Godhead, He is omnipotent having the power to raise Christ from the dead and He will raise all mankind from their graves at the resurrection. The Holy Ghost is omnipresent having the ability to be in all places at all times. Therefore, He is capable of the judgment of all mankind; because He has a first-hand eyewitness to all that mankind ever does. Jehovah God and Jesus Christ communicate with the Holy Ghost; because He searches our minds and God and Christ knows what is in our minds through the Holy Ghost. God and Christ know every thought and intent of mankind's hearts or minds. The Holy Ghost is also omniscient knowing the past, present, and future; thereby, the Holy Ghost also searches the profound things of Jehovah God and He knows the things of God. For what man knows the stuff of a man, except the spirit of man which is in Him.

The secret to the great mystery of how can a grown man or woman be born again of God? With mankind, this is impossible, but with Jehovah God this is possible. To be born again of God and not of man, we must be born again of the Spirit of God, through water Baptism, for the forgiveness of our sins and thereby, we will receive from Jehovah God the Holy Spirit who regenerates us by the renewing of our minds. The Holy Spirit of God lives in Christians who obey the commandments of the New Testament, and He will not live in the bodies of the sinners and ungodly of this world. The Holy Spirit who lives in Christians is our teacher and our leader; thereby, He teaches us the Scriptures, and He leads us in the paths of righteousness. He also helps us with our physical and moral weaknesses to overcome them by temptations of our flesh. He will provide us a way to escape these temptations, so we do not sin. A holy spirit is a spirit person, because He is invisible to the human eye. The Holy Bible is not the Holy Spirit, but the Bible is the work of the Holy Spirit, and all the Bible are the oracles of Jehovah God's mouth.

Chapter Fourteen
God, the Father of All, and Above All, in Heaven and Earth

The helpful guidance of Jehovah god toward his children that serve Him here on earth is similar to that in heaven. At the beginning of America, our forefathers founded our religion upon serving Jehovah God. And they established our constitution, and our laws of our land are based upon the principles of the Holy Scriptures. Therefore, Jehovah God blessed our nation from every direction under the heavens. God opened the windows of heaven and poured manifold blessings upon our Christian nation. Many have lost their way in America and wandered off the path of serving our Living God, but God has not given up on our great nation.

The key to understanding the Holy Scriptures about Jehovah God, you first must realize that God is the supreme, almighty Living God in heaven and He has everyone working for Him that serves Him. Jehovah God tells the Holy Ghost, Jesus Christ, and all the holy angels what He wants to be done. God tells them what to do and what to say; this makes all the works of Jesus Christ, Holy Ghost, and the holy angels at His command and they perform His will.

Jehovah God has appointed a new president in America that believes upon Him, and He has restored by eliminating the laws that were made contrary to the requirements of God. Now our country will be blessed again, as it was in the beginning and like Israel was under the reign of King David in Israel. God expanded the kingdom of David, and He was the greatest King in Israel; because God built up Israel under his rule, and God brought down the enemies of Israel. God healed the brokenhearted and bound up their wounds. God lifts up the humble and cast down the wicked to the ground. God takes pleasure in all those who fear Him and hope in His Mercy. God made the walls and gates of the city of Jerusalem strong and He blessed the people in the town. God made peace with Israel's enemies and filled them with the finest wheat. Jehovah God proclaims this blessing upon every mankind who walks not in the counsel of the ungodly, not stands in the path of sinners, nor sits in the seats of the scornful; but his delight is in the laws of the Lord, and in His law, he meditates day and night. He shall be like a tree planted beside a river of water, that brings forth its fruit in season, whose leaves shall not wither, and whatsoever He doeth, He shall prosper.

Jehovah God is the father of everyone in heaven and on earth; because he is their creator in the beginning. Jesus Christ is the very first person that God Created in heaven, Jesus declared, "I am the beginning of the creation of God."

Who makes Jesus the firstborn son of God and all angels and all Mankind who serve Jehovah God faithfully are called the sons of God, because we are the children of God.

Therefore, the head of Christ is Jehovah God, because when God gave Jesus Christ all power in heaven and on earth to rule over them until the end of earth time. God excepted his power out of that commandment he gave Jesus. Therefore, when Christians pray, they direct their prayers to God, but must ask for the petitions in the name of Jesus Christ to receive the request from God. Jesus Christ throne is on the right-hand side of Jehovah God's throne in heaven and when Christians slip and fall by committing a sin, we confess and repent of the crime and pray to God for forgiveness, asking in the name of Jesus Christ; for Jesus is our advocate with the Father on our behalf, because Jesus Christ is our reconciliation with God when our sin separates us from Him. Jehovah God sent Jesus Christ into the world to be a propitiation for mankind's sins that our faith in His bloodshed on the cross, Jesus could reconcile us to God.

The ways that Jehovah God worked through Jesus Christ is on this wise. When God and His Spirit lived alone in heaven, God became creative, and the very first thing that God created was His first begotten son, Jesus Christ. God made him in his image and likeness with the same mindset as God Himself. Then God created all the other angels of heaven, and God exalted Jesus higher than the angels in heaven and made Jesus part of the Godhead, and He ruled over them. Then God created all the planets, all the stars, and the earth also; but the earth was covered with waters, and it remained that way for about six hundred billion years, according to carbon dating by mankind and all the while

Jesus shared with God the glories of heaven and being the ruler over the angels in heaven. After about six hundred billion years had passed, according to the measurement of time, Jehovah God began to create the earth so that it could support the lives of mankind. Then God created everything on earth, though, by and for his son, Jesus Christ.

During the period of Moses and the prophets, Jehovah God sent Jesus Christ down to earth, many times to visit with Moses, Abraham, and some of the prophets. Then when Israel lost their way in serving God and the gentile people were living without a covenant relationship with God, whereby they could save their souls. The time had come with Jehovah God that He sent his son, Jesus Christ, into the world, down through the descendants of Adam, down through the bloodlines of Virgin Mary. The birth of Jesus was on this wise when the Holy Ghost of God, through the operation of incarnation, performed the miraculous task of making Virgin Mary pregnant with Jesus, whose became the son of God and the son of man. Because God wanted Jesus to create a new covenant with mankind, whereby all mankind could have a plan of salvation for their souls and not just the Jewish people only. When Jesus was baptized in the River of Jordan, God sent down the Holy Ghost from heaven and He went inside the body of Jesus Christ, giving Him the power of God and giving Jesus every word that is written in the New Covenant.

When Jesus Christ died on the Cross, according to the plan of his father, Jehovah God, in heaven. God commanded the Holy Ghost to raise Jesus from the dead on the third day. But while Jesus lay in the tomb, by the power

97

of the Holy Ghost Jesus Spirit went and defeated Satan here on earth and took him to the prison of hell, to await the final judgment, whereby Jesus will put him in the Lake of Fire. Then the Holy Ghost raised Jesus body from the dead, He spent forty days and nights with his apostles, teaching them of the things to come. Then Jehovah God brought Jesus Christ back to heaven and sat him back upon the same throne that He left when He came to earth. Now God has anointed Jesus Christ with all the power and rule in heaven and on earth until the end of earth time. But God is still the Father in His own house and He accepted His power out of the control that God bestowed upon Jesus. So the order of the Godhead is on this wise, Jehovah God is the supreme ruler over all, Jesus Christ is the ruler of all the angels in heaven and all mankind upon the earth, and the Holy Ghost is the spirit of God and Christ, and He is at their command. God also gave Jesus Christ the power and responsibility to judge the lives of all mankind on the earth. Jesus will use the old scriptures to judge the people who lived under that covenant and Jesus will apply the New Testament of scriptures to judge the people who live under that covenant. This is all the contracts between the true living God and mankind.

Jehovah God and Jesus Christ work through the Holy Ghost, who is the spirit of God, on this wise. The Holy Ghost is the third person in the Godhead, and He is the source of power for them; the Holy Ghost is at their command. The Holy Ghost is an eye and ear witness for God and Christ on earth; because He has the power to be in all places at all times. Therefore, He knows everything and every word that mankind will speak or do, so God has appointed the Holy Ghost to be the witness of every person that ever lived upon the earth, for every single day we live. The Holy Ghost will justify or condemn every soul that comes before Jesus Christ on the Day of Judgment. The Holy Ghost lives in the bodies of Christians and He relays our prayers to God in heaven, even our silent prayers. He helps us with our mental or physical weaknesses and He leads us in the paths of righteousness, He helps us understand the Scriptures. And many other things He does to help Christians here on Earth. The world of sinners and the ungodly cannot receive the Holy Ghost, for He will not live in their sinful bodies; but He will condemn them because He is in every place in the world at the same time.

Jehovah God and Jesus Christ work through the holy angels, and they sometimes are referred to as messengers of God. The angels of God have appeared to many of God's people in the Old Testament with messages from God. They appeared to Abraham, Balaam, Daniel, King David, Elijah, Hagar, Jacob, Moses, Lot, Manoah, and wife, Zechariah.

There are many witnesses in the New Testament of the holy angels and they appeared to Apostle John, Paul, Peter, Philip, and God sent them to help Jesus when He was on earth to support Jesus in His ministry, and appeared to many other people in the Bible. God appointed angels to minister to the Christians in the first seven churches. The angels were ministers to the saints in the Old Testament times, and they are still ministers to Christians in the New Testament times. Jesus said in Matthew, Chapter Eighteen, verse ten, *that angels are guardians of God's children*. And they look over and protect those who believe in Him. For this reason, we must teach our children when they are very young the

Scriptures and give them faith in our living God and Jesus Christ. My mother taught me the scriptures from about the age of five years old and it was her that gave me my faith in God that led to the saving of my soul.

The key to knowledge in the Holy Scriptures of the living Jehovah God and He is the source of mankind's knowledge and wisdom, because God is the father thereof. The key of knowledge to understanding God is on this wise; God owns everything, for without Him, there would be nothing, He is the creator of all thing in heaven and on earth; therefore, all belongs to God. Jesus commanded that Christians worship God and when we pray to God, ask our petitions in His name, because He is our advocate for us with God, and He will do it for us. Christians worship Jesus Christ in our memorial service of communing with him through breaking of the bread and drinking the new wine, just as Jesus did with his disciples in the lord's *the last supper* with them.

The key to mankind's wisdom to understanding our living Jehovah God and how He works His Godhead is on this wise. Think, how would the American federal government function, if we only had the president to rule over the federal government, without any cabinet leaders to help him? How could the president of a big corporation, like Walmart, function with just the president to manage the whole company? Our Living Jehovah God employs in heaven to help Him, His son, Jesus Christ, His holy spirit, and His holy angels. Jehovah God operates on earth to help him, Jesus Christ, his son, His Holy Spirit, his holy angels. In our living god's kingdom here on Earth, which is his church that Jesus established and Apostle Peter opened.

Jesus set in the kingdom some apostles, and some prophets, and some evangelists, some pastors, and teachers. Then after the churches was established and opened, Jesus had the apostles to ordain elders and deacons to help operate the churches.

Chapter Fifteen

God Hears and Answers Prayers According to His Will

There was a particular man that I knew that I had not seen in a while. He came into the store where I worked and He looks sad and downtrodden. So I asked him how was he doing. He said that his wife came down sick and died, and He prayed and prayed to God to heal wife and let her live, but God would not help him? Well, I was shocked, and I said, "Where do you go to church, did you have the whole church praying to God on your behalf?"

And he said, "I used to go to church about fifteen years ago, but we quit going to church."

Well, I said, "Do you not know the Scriptures?"

"Where?" God said. "Do not forsake the assembling of going to church, for this is a willful sin against God, and He has removed the blood of his son, Jesus Christ, from cleansing your sins."

Now you only have the judgment to look forward to and the fiery indignation of God, which shall devour his adversaries. It is a fearful thing to fall into the hands of our Living God for judgment.

When I asked this man to go back to church and make it right with God, He refused my pleas for him to seek God. Jesus warns people to seek the kingdom of God first, which is the church and He will add all your needs unto you. If you forsake God, He will forsake you, and if you deny God, He will reject you. Our sins separates us from our living Jehovah God, and when separated from God, He will not answer our prayers, as long as we are sinners or ungodly person. But when we love God and obey His commandments, He hears our every prayer, because His eyes are over the righteous and His ears are open to hearing their prayers; but the face of the Lord God is against them that do evil. God will not answer any prayer that is against His will to grant us our request. Whosoever hath and they see their needy brothers and sisters here on earth are in need of food and clothing and they harden their hearts and not hear of their cry for help; God will also not hear your prayers for relief. Anyone who turns away their ear from listening to and obeying the Laws of God and His ministers here on earth, their prayers to God will be an abomination to God.

Jehovah God will not hear the prayers of the sinners and the ungodly people of this world. God will not answer any prayer that you ask him; if you consume it upon the lust of your flesh, the desire of your eyes, or for the pride of your life. God will not give you anything that will cause harm to come to you or if there is anything wrong with you having what you prayed. God will not provide you with anything if you have doubts that He is not able to perform your prayers or if you have any doubts whatsoever. We must believe that

God is ready and we are worthy to receive the petitions that we make to Him.

If you love God, He will love you, and if you hate God, He will laugh at you when calamity comes upon you. If you forsake God, He will leave you; but if you seek God, you will find God. If you knock on His door, He will open the gate unto you.

If you love God, you will prove it by keeping His commandments, and He will like you. God will treasure up in heaven all your prayers as a memorial to you. We must be sincere and specific in our prayer requests to God, and we must have the faith that we will receive them from God.

Jehovah God will hear the prayers of the righteous people of a nation. If they will humble themselves and pray to God to forgive their sins and seek Him with tears of sorrow or remorse for the sins and turn away from their wicked ways, God will hear them from heaven and He will forgive their sins and heal their nation. Christians have set aside a particular day every year to pray to God for the nation's sins and mourn for their lost souls that perhaps they may turn and serve God. We must keep the commandments of the New Testament to be a righteous Christian. We must forgive others of their trespasses against us because God will not forgive us of our trespasses against others when we pray and ask His forgiveness.

There is a particular church, and a member of that congregation told me that there was a sister of their congregation who came down with cancer in several parts of her body. The whole church brought her before the assembly including the elder's, preacher, deacons, and all the member's, and they all prayed earnestly with faith that

God would heal her, and when she went back to the doctor, the cancer was almost gone completely. God commands all Christians if any are afflicted, then let them pray to God, and if any are happy, sing a song unto the Lord. And if any are sick, let them call for the elders of the church; and let them pray over them, anointing them with oil in the name of the Lord, and the prayer of faith shall save the sick, and the Lord shall raise them up; and if they have committed sins, they shall be forgiven. The effectual fervent prayers of a righteous man availeth much.

Look what God had done when Elijah prayed to him earnestly that it would not rain on the earth for forty-two months; then He prayed again that God would send the rains and He opened the heavens and poured rain upon the earth, and the earth gave people its fruits. Moreover, when Elijah had the contest with the false prophets of Baal and his living God Jehovah to see who would answer their prayer's. Whosoever responded to their prayers, they would be the true God. Mostly all Israel was serving the false God and had forsaken the living God. Elijah took the four hundred and fifty prophets to the mountaintop of Mountain Carmel, and He rebuilt the altar that had fallen, where the Israelis formerly worshipped Jehovah God. Then He built the false prophets an alter and put wood on them with a bull to sacrifice to their Gods. Then Elijah told the 450 false prophets of Baal to ask their God to send down from heaven fire and burn their sacrifice. They prayed all day calling upon a God who had no ears, no eyes, no mouth, no intelligence, no life in them and he never answered. Then, late in the day, after Elijah made fun of their false god, he told them to bring five barrels full of water and pour upon the altar and fill the trench around the platform with water, making it hard for his Living God. Then Elijah prayed earnestly to the Living God Jehovah to send down from heaven fire and burn his sacrifice and God heard him and sent down fire and it consumed the bull, the altar, and licked up all the five barrels of water around the altar.

Jehovah God did not pity the false prophets of Baal who pulled away from his servants from him to worship their false god. Jehovah God had Elijah take the 450 false prophets down off the mountain to a brook and Elijah slew them with his sword. The supporters of these 450 false prophets was King Ahab and Queen Jezebelle and they met horrible deaths. What remains were left of Jezebelle the dogs came and devoured her. Jehovah God will put all false prophets, preachers, teachers and all who serve false gods into hell when they die and at the end of time, He will put them into the Lake of Fire that burns with brimstones. God hates liars and falsehoods because Satan is the father of all such evil deeds.

Our prayer's that we make to our Living Jehovah God they are every Christian's duty. Prayers are the medium of access to our relationship with our living God. Christians must ask all their prayers in the name of Jesus Christ to receive anything from Jehovah God; because Jesus is our advocate with the father, and He will pray to the father all our prayers on our behalf.

The key to knowledge of understanding how Jehovah God makes the decision of answering our prayers to Him is likened unto a father who built his wife and ten children a beautiful mansion to live in and it came to pass that five of his children loved him very much and they adored their father. Whatsoever their father assigned them to accomplish, they have done it wholeheartedly with all their might. But the other five children, they would not obey their father and they did not respect him. Those five children became overtaken and possessed by Satan, and they became very evil and done wickedness all the days of their lives. Their father loved all ten of his children and he worried what may come upon them in this life and what would happen to them in the life to come. These five evil children were involved in gambling, narcotics, rioter's, haters of other people, and haters of Jehovah God. They were unthankful, unholy, without natural affection in their hearts. Now it came to pass that their father was getting very old and sick, He wanted to make a will and name the five children that loved and obeyed him, to be heirs of the mansion and all his kingdom, but the five children that despised him and would not obey him; he left them out of his will and they received their portion with Satan. And so it is with our Heavenly Father, those children of the earth that love and obey Him will inherit the mansion in the Kingdom of Heaven and those children of the earth that hate him and disobey him in their evil and wicked ways, they will inherit hell and the Lake of Fire, forever and ever.

Chapter Sixteen
The Priceless Bounties of Our Heavenly Father

The generosity of our Heavenly Father whose name is Jehovah God is not known among mankind. His generous gifts and rewards to mankind are unequal and priceless. Consider the gift of salvation of our souls; what would you profit if you gained the whole world, and lose your soul? Or what would you give in exchange for your soul? Well, if we owned the whole world and everything in the world and gave it to God, it would not repay the debt we owe God for the salvation of our soul.

How much does God love mankind? He gave his only begotten son to suffer at the hands of sinful man and be put to death by crucifixion on the Cross in order to give all mankind a better plan of Salvation of our souls. By his death, mankind received the holy gospels of Jesus Christ whereby we can be saved. Before this, only the Jews could be saved, all others were excluded in the Old Testament. When we follow God's plan of salvation as outlined in the New Testaments and we walk in the truth of God's word, we are called the Children of God, thereby, God is our heavenly father just as He is Jesus Christ's heavenly father. This gift is priceless, because the benefits to the Christians are so valuable. God hears and answers our prayers, He forgives our sins when we repent of them, and He gives us good gifts to enjoy on earth all the days of our Christian life. God loves and protects us like our earthly fathers and mothers.

Blessed is the person that does not walk in the counsels of the ungodly or the sinners, or associates with the scornful of the earth, but their delight is in the laws of the Lord Jesus Christ and thereby, they meditate in them day and night being a doer of his words. God will make you likened unto a tree which is planted by the rivers of water, which will bring forth fruit in season and the leaves will not wither and whatsoever, they will do God will prosper them on every side. The ungodly this is not so; they will be like a wave driven in the sea and tossed away and they will not stand before God in the Day of Judgment, nor will the sinners who can't quit sinning.

Blessed are the people who are humble and kind in spirit; for theirs is the Kingdom of Heaven. Blessed are the meek and lowly; for they shall inherit the New Earth. Blessed are those who mourn; for they shall be comforted. Blessed are they which do hunger and thirst after righteousness; for they shall be filled. Blessed are the people who are merciful to others; for they shall obtain mercy from God. Blessed are those who are pure in heart; for they shall see God in heaven. Blessed are the people who are peacemakers; for they shall be called the children of God. Blessed are they who are persecuted for righteousness' sake; for theirs is the Kingdom of Heaven.

Blessed are the Christians when others revile and persecute you, and say all manner of evil against you falsely for Jesus Christ's sake. Rejoice and be exceedingly glad; for great is your reward in heaven. These *blessings* are priceless from our living God who spoke these through his beloved son, Jesus Christ, for they cannot be purchased with money.

God gave Christians the power to defeat Satan through his son Jesus Christ's work while his body lay dead in the grave. By God's spirit, Jesus Christ spirit came forth from his body and they defeated Satan and his angels that followed him and put them into hell awaiting the final judgment day which they will spend eternity in the Lake of Fire. Today, Satan only has the power that people give him in their lives. Satan does not make us do anything that we don't want to do today. This gift cannot be purchased with money.

God's gift to mankind is grace which He sent to us through His son, Jesus Christ. This grace is when mankind believes in the New Covenant and they are baptized for the forgiveness of all their past sins, God forgives every sin they ever committed during their lives to this time. Wow! This is amazing grace, we have never done anything to deserve this grace but believe and repent of our sins. But after this, we must be a doer of the word of God and we must repent of each and every sin that we commit and do them no more; for we are saved by our faith and our works in our judgment.

Our God will supply all Christian's needs according to His riches in glory by Christ Jesus. When we need wisdom to understand the Bible or wisdom for any occasion, we ask God in prayer and He will give wisdom to us very liberally if we do not doubt God. For if we doubt God in anything,

He will not give us anything. Did you ever read anywhere in the Bible where Jesus Christ has done anything for anyone who did not believe in Him? We must have faith in God in order to please God. If any Christian is sick, we go to God in prayer and ask in the name of Jesus Christ and if we have faith that God will heal us; if it is God's will, He will heal us of our sicknesses. I have heard of Christians being sick with cancer and they bring them upfront of the congregation and have the elders, preachers, deacons and all the members pray for them. And the prayers of faith shall save the sick, and the Lord shall raise them up, and if they have committed sins, they shall be forgiven them. The effectual fervent prayers of the righteous availed much.

O the bounties of my living Jehovah God are so wonderful and mighty, may I testify to you how much I believe and love Him? My mother taught me the New Testament since I was five years old and I believed them because my Christian mother believed them. I loved God because God loved poor people who believed and loved Him like in the rich man and Lazarus story. Our family was also very poor but we were taught a work ethic and about God.

God saved me from a wild boar and a rattlesnake that was ready to strike me, which was about six feet above me on a mountainside. God saved me when I was sick unto death with chicken pox, measles, and mumps with a temperature of about 106 degrees. My parent's thought this was my last day on earth, but God heard my prayers and sent my guardian angel from heaven to heal me and show me in a vision the actual Lake of Fire that will come on the earth on the last day of time.

When I was eighteen years old, God saved me from death in a car wreck which was totaled. When I was doing ninety-five miles an hour in a 1949 Buick, which hit a solid rock cliff, and the car had done three turnovers in the air landing on its top sliding down the highway about two hundred feet. I never got a scratch in the wreck because God heard my prayer and answered them. Wow! How much do I love and believe in God with all my being.

When I was forty years old, God saved me from being killed by two armed robbers who had, beforehand, killed their father for insurance money and escaped from prison. They robbed the store I managed and took me hostage. When we were getting in the getaway car, I knew all hostages taken in robberies get killed, so I refused to get in the car. One of the robbers pointed his gun at me and said, "You get in the car, or I will kill you."

I prayed to God to save me and not allow this man to shoot me and God saved me from death again. They got into the car and got away with the money, leaving me behind.

When I was sixty-eight years old, God sent the same angel that visited me in 1950, which healed me and showed me the Lake of Fire in a vision. God was upset with me for not living up to my vows that I made to him in 1950 when I was sick unto death. I had promised when I became an old man that I would do something that He would be very proud of me for doing. But in fact He was displeased with me for committing sins and not repenting for them. Moreover, God was displeased with our nation that once was a strong nation who served Him; but now had drifted away from serving Him in immorality. And all the sins that the people were doing on the other side of the flood which God destroyed them.

I communicated with my God in heaven through the angel who told me when I talked to him I was talking to God because God heard me and God told him what to say to me. Thereby, I communicated with our Living God for about thirty minutes and Jesus Christ asked me a question near the end of the visit. God asked me through the angel if I knew and could tell him why our country has come to the place that we find ourselves in today. After I gave the best answer I could, God chastised me for making a false accusation in my prayers saying God gave me unlawful women and not staying away from them.

Well, I began to cry and feeling ashamed of myself for letting God down in my vows and committing these sins. I repented to God with tears, telling God how sorry I was for my sins and I believed in Him and loved Him more than anyone in heaven or on earth. God forgave me of my sins, wrote my name back into the Book of Life in heaven. God forgave me of a sin that I worried about from time to time and another sin, He didn't think I knew was a sin to commit.

Chapter Seventeen

God, the Father of Good and Life, but Satan, the Father of Evil and Death

The evil god of this world, whose name is Satan, and all the wrong people who follow after the evil and wickedness of Satan, the same as the ones that cause bad things to happen to people. Look what happened to Sodom and Gomorrah when Satan and all the wicked people of those countries committed every evil and wicked sin known to man. They would not repent and Jehovah God passed judgment upon those countries and wiped them off the face of the earth.

Look what happened to the city of Nineveh who committed so much evil that Jehovah God sent the Prophet Jonah into the great city to preach against the wickedness of the people. Jehovah God gave the people forty days to repent, or He would overthrow the city and destroy them all. The people believed Jonah and the king of that great city put on mourning sackcloth and sat down in ashes. And the king proclaimed and published throughout Nineveh by the decree of the king and the nobles. He forbade every person and every animal of the city, not to eat or drink anything;

but let mankind and beast all be covered with the sackcloth and pray to the mighty living God Jehovah. Let all people turn from the violence that they have done, for who can tell if God will repent and turn away from his anger, that we perish not; and God saw their work, which they had turned from their evil ways, and God did repent himself of the evil that he had said he would do unto them and he did it not.

Now the Christians of the world have a great battle to fight, which is a spiritual battle against Satan and the bad people who follow after his wickedness here on earth. These evil people commit all manner of evil and wicked sins, and they deny the son of God, Jesus Christ. Satan's children use every weapon in Satan's arsenal to fight against the Christians of the world. They exceed the wickedness of the people before the great flood that God used to destroy the world, except Noah and his family, which was denying Jehovah God and now deny Jesus Christ, they worshipped false gods, and they rejected the living God. They change the Scriptures into lies. They dishonored their bodies between themselves, without natural affection of love in their hearts for other people and have no respect for those who rule over them. Moreover, have a reprobate mind filled with all manner of unrighteousness and wickedness. They are without any understanding, and they have no self-control of their actions, they have no mercy for any other person on earth, they are full of lies and deceits and false reports. They are covenant breakers of all manner of legal contracts made between mankind. Their mind is continually thinking of ways they can extort money from other people or cause others pain and misery in their lives.

Christians must rise and try to pull these types of evil people out of the jaws of eternal hell and Lake of Fire and separate yourselves from them. We must return to serving Jehovah God with a vengeance because we are over 2,000 years closer to the end of time than we were when Jesus Christ came to earth. Our living Jehovah God has that date set, and Jesus Christ is ready to return for the Judgment Day when God approves.

Jesus told the rich young ruler that came to him and asked, "Good Master, what good thing can I do to inherit eternal life?"

Jesus replied, "Why call me 'Good'? There is none good except God."

Jehovah God, our living God, He is good all the time, in Him is no evil whatsoever. Jehovah God has warned every soul in the whole world what his laws are in the Holy Bible, *"Do not deceive yourselves, when you break these laws of Jehovah God, He gives you a specific time to repent and turn from those sins, and if we fail to repent, God will pass His judgment against us with punishment for the crime's that we have done. Be not deceived, no one mocks God by sinning, and think they can get away with them; whatsoever we sow in this life, we shall reap the harvest of what crime we have sown."*

When Satan and one-third of the angels in heaven attempted to overthrow Jehovah God and become the rulers of heaven, they lost the battle and God cast out of heaven down to the earth. At this time, Satan had great powers, and he wreaked havoc upon the people of the earth for centuries. Satan tempted and lied to Eve, deceiving her to disobey the commandment from her living Jehovah God, thereby God

116

cast Adam and Eve out of the eternal Garden of Eden. God cursed Eve with the burden of bearing children, being the keeper of the home, and her desires would be unto her husband. And then God cursed Adam, commanding that He would have to work and make their living from the fruit of the ground by the sweat of his face until they returned to the ground from where they created. Satan caused mankind to receive the death penalty for the sins of our beginning father and mother of humankind.

Satan then entered into mankind and persuaded them to commit sins of worshipping idols and not worship their living God who created them. They became vain in their foolish minds, professing themselves to be wise people who became evil and wicked fools. Then worshipped false gods, they burned with sexual lust in the bodies, becoming homosexuals and lesbians, dishonoring their bodies among themselves. Then changed the words of God, which is the truth, into their lies. They misused the Scriptures just as Satan has always done with mankind. Now because Satan had caused the people to drift away from serving God through their vile affections toward one another, He gave them over to a reprobate mind. God gave up on trying to convert them to help Him. Because they were haters of God, inventors of evil things, malicious against one another, full of all wickedness and unrighteousness that Satan has in his arsenal to destroy humankind. God passed judgment and gave Noah 120 years to build an ark to save his family and one male and one female of all His creation in the ark. Then God opened the windows of heaven and poured rain upon the earth forty days and nights, destroying all the ungodly of the world with a flood. Jehovah God tried to rid the world of all unrighteousness and begin anew with the righteous seed of mankind.

God began the new world after the flood with Noah and his sons, Ham, Shem, and Japeth, and after 2,348 years of repopulation of the Earth, that it came to pass that mankind became very wicked again. Jehovah God became very dissatisfied with mankind and this created with God, the acceptable time to send his beloved son, Jesus Christ, into the world to make a new covenant with mankind. Until then, the Old Covenant was with the Jewish people only, and God wanted a new covenant to include all people of the earth. When Jesus came to earth, Satan had so much power over people that Jehovah God called Satan *the God of This World* and *the Prince of Devils,* because he ruled over them. Some examples of Satan's power in the New Testament was the time Satan had a legion of his angels to enter into a Gadarenes man, and they drove him out of his mind. Satan came into one of Jesus Christ's disciples, whose name was Judas, and Satan led Judas to betray the Lord for thirty pieces of silver. Then Satan prompted Judas to hang himself until death. Satan entered into a man named Ananias and his wife, Sapphira, and caused them to lie to the Holy Ghost. God called Satan, The Ruler of Sin, because he perverts the truth to people, he oppresses people, he opposes the works of God, he is the father of all lies, deceits, false reports, he appears as an angel and blinds the minds of believers, he is the adversary to all mankind. Satan is the father of murder; look what he did to job, he smote job with boils from the soles of his feet to the top of his head, he killed all jobs children. Satan attends worship services, and he misuses the Scriptures, and he supports evil people.

The key of knowledge of understanding which causes bad things to happen to people on the earth is to study the Holy Bible and become a servant to Jehovah God in his kingdom, which is his church here on earth. Learn that it is the God of this world, Satan that is the Father of all evil and ungodly acts committed against their fellow mankind. Then become a Christian and pray to God to give you the wisdom to understand all the Scriptures; learning that it is Jehovah God who is the God of all goodness, mercy, and all righteousness to everyone on earth.

Whatsoever a person soweth, that shall he also reap in this life. God has a natural law built into all people of the earth. Examples of this law are on this wise. If we commit sexual immorality, we may come down sick with a social disease. If we become an alcoholic or drug addict, we may suffer from many sicknesses and many personal losses. If we commit gluttony, we may become obese. If we commit various crimes, we may receive in our bodies a different punishment than we determined, but all people who live by violence against others will die from violence themselves.

The key to wisdom of the causes of bad things happening to people on earth is on this wise. Bad things happen to innocent people when evil people commit acts of violence against them. Bad things happen to people when they break the laws of the land or commit crimes. Sicknesses occur to people because of the sins committed by Adam and Eve, and God pronounced they would surely die someday and not live forever here on earth in the Garden of Eden. Therefore, God made our bodies to wear out in old age and cause us to come down with various diseases and cause us to die.

Chapter Eighteen
Sinners and Ungodly Will Go Away into Everlasting Punishment at Death

Jehovah God does love everyone, but He hates the sins that people commit. The Bible gives us great examples, He loved all the angels that He made in heaven, but about one-third of them rebelled against God and wanted to overthrow Him. So God had to deal with the unexpected event and He threw them out of heaven and cast them down to earth as a temporary fix to his problem. Then God had to make a permanent holding place for Satan and all his angels that followed him also a holding place for all the people on earth that rebelled against Him and would not obey Him. God tells us in the fourth chapter of Ephesians that Jesus when he died on the Cross, that while he lay in the tomb, his spirit descended down into the lower parts of the earth. According to a certain man who is a friend and brother in the lord told me of his vision that Jesus showed him hell and it was in the lower parts of the earth.

In the first book of Apostle Peter, in chapter three, he tells us that when Jesus was in the tomb, that he took Satan and all his angels that followed him, who lived on earth, in the bodies of evil people. Jesus took all them down into the lower parts of the earth, to the place called "Hell." There, Jesus preached a sermon to the lost spirits that was in hell who disobeyed God before the great flood and Jesus threw Satan and all his angel's into hell with the lost souls of mankind. Jesus called this place a prison for the lost souls and they are sentenced by Jehovah God to stay in that prison of hell until the end of earth time comes and then they are transferred to The Lake of Fire to live there forever and ever without end.

In the Scriptures of the second Peter, chapter three, God tells us of the place that the Lake of Fire will be. Now I testify before everyone on earth and everyone in heaven, that God showed me in a vision The Lake of Fire. The entire story is written in my book called *The Lake of Fire Is Real and Here on Earth* published by West Bow Press. In the year of 1950 at the age of seven, I came down sick unto death and Jehovah God heard my crying prayers to save me from death and He sent my Guardian angel from heaven to heal me completely and to show me in a vision The Lake of Fire. And it was here on earth right where the Scriptures tell us, I am an eye and ear-witness to this fact. The angel of God took my spirit high above my home on Browns Fork, Kentucky in Perry County, near Hazard, Kentucky and showed me the actual Lake of Fire.

This is what the Lake of Fire looked like. The whole world was on fire as far as my eyes could see and the flames were burning all over the world with creamy white flames, that was at least 100 feet high, with yellow colors around the edges of the flames, and silky black smoke was ascending up into the heavens of the flames. When I looked up into the heavens, it was so silky black dark from the smoke. I could not see the moon, sun, or any stars in the heavens. This scared me and I began to cry and the angel must have shaken me, then I heard two women coming across midfield of the seven-acre farm that my family planted every year.

One woman said, "I don't know why God put me in here, I was a good woman all my life, I never did anything really bad, but I never went to church and served Him."

And the other woman said, "I am like you, but before God done this to earth, I had plenty of wealth, but I am so hot in these flames, I would give all the wealth that I owned for one glass of water. God had my spirit encased in a crystal-clear case and as I looked around at the earth where I lived. I could not see our home or the barn and daddy's truck that he parked near the barn."

All the elements of the earth were being dissolved in the flames that will burn with fire and brimstones that Jesus will rain down upon the earth at the end of time. These Flames had dissolved all the elements as far as my eyes could see and the waters of the creek that ran down in front of my home were all gone, just like the Scriptures said they would be. I heard other people down below me in the Lake of Fire, and I heard some grinding on their teeth, some were hollering sounds of pain and misery. The Lake of Fire is eight-time hotter than hell.

My mother gave me a great answer when I asked her this question, "Mommy, why does God have a place called hell? I thought that He loved everyone."

"Well, Jerry," she said, "right here on Browns Fork Hollow, you have Men that have killed one another, and you have men that has taken women to the top of the mountains and rape them and beat them, leaving them for dead. When God brings you to heaven, do you want these people living in heaven with you?"

I answered this question immediately and said, "No, I don't mind putting up with them here on earth, But if God brings me to heaven, I don't want them up there with me."

Now I understood very plainly why God has an eternal home for good people and a different eternal home for evil people when we die and at the end of time.

God named the place of the saved people heaven because the way that God explains the eternal home for all the saved people is a place to be desired. Living in mansions, walking on streets made of pure gold. The citizens of the Kingdom of Heaven living together in unity, love, and peace with one another; everyone living forever and never get sick or die and we will have a heavenly body that is equal to the angels who are in heaven. We will all rest from our labor that we have to do here on earth, because God will give us everything we need free of charge. Everyone who now have mental or physical disabilities having none of these things in heaven. Because our inner person that is our spirit will be given a heavenly body, which will live forever. The weather in heaven will be sunshine for all eternity, there will be no severe weather in heaven. There will be no racism in heaven, no riots, no hatred, no envy, and every citizen of heaven will all be treated equally in heaven, because all the wealth and all the power and authority of people on earth today will be left behind to be destroyed and God will make all things new in heaven and all will be rich in heaven.

The keys of knowledge to understanding why Jehovah God's will is for all mankind upon the earth is told to us by His beloved son, Jesus Christ, in the New Testament. Matthew 5:43-48, *"Jesus commands Christians to love everyone upon the earth, the evil people, as well as the good people."*

God wants us also to try to convert them to serve God, saving their unworthy souls, as an evil doer. God makes his sun to shine on the evil and on the good, He also sends rain on the just and unjust. When everyone is born, God has determined and appointed their allotted days that we all have to spend on this earth until we pass away in death. Therefore, Jehovah God does not intervene in the lives of mankind, to make us all good, therein wiping out any evil-doers upon the earth. However, God gave mankind a choice to live their lives doing good or doing evil, we are all, our free moral agents.

The Scriptures give us great prime examples of people who have done evil and been converted to do good. The best example is a man named Saul, a Pharisee in his religion who went about the earth beating and murdering people of the Christian faith. Now Jehovah God and Jesus Christ hated the evil deeds that Saul was committing against his Christians. However, God knows what everyone does on earth all the allotted days of our lives on earth. God knew that if Jesus appeared in the heavens to Saul while he was on the road to Damascus to kill Christians, that Saul would repent and serve the true Living Jehovah God and not serve Satan by his evil deeds, Acts 9:1-31. Saul changed his name to Paul after baptism into the Kingdom of God and he became a preacher for Jesus, and the Pharisees plotted to kill him. Now Apostle Paul became the hardest working apostle of all, because he owed God the most significant amount of debt for forgiving Saul of all the many grievous sins that he committed, which God hated.

The key of wisdom to understanding why Jehovah God has a place called hell and a place called The Lake of Fire is on this wise. The answer to this question lies within every human that ever lived on this earth. Suppose you obey all the commandments written in the New Testament and you die and go to heaven. Would you want God also to save the people who are murders, rapist, child molesters, troublemakers, Racists, God-haters, ungodly, people who have no self-control, people who hate others, people without love in their hearts, drunkards and drug addicts, and people who hate anyone in authority over them.

Chapter Nineteen

The Righteous Will Live Forever in the New Heaven and New Earth

The benefits of serving the almighty living Jehovah God is without measure and exceeds the imagination of mankind, because his gifts to mankind that serve Him are more valuable than all the wealth in the whole earth. God said by the mouth of His Apostle Paul, look at all the goodness and all the severity of God. His Goodness he bestows upon the good people of the earth and His severity He bestows upon the evil people of this world.

The benefits of serving God here on earth, for as long as we live here is awesome. We Christian's receive the peace that comes from being the children of our eternal father who is in heaven; therefore, we have the rest that comes from our Lord Jesus Christ that he gave freely to all that accept and serve his father God in heaven. All who serve God has sweet rest and sleep, because our mind is free from hatred of others, and we have no fear of the police and authorities who rule over us on the earth, we obey the laws of our country if they are not against the laws of our living God.

God gives us the ability to work and gives us our talents, because He commanded that man to work and earned his living to support his family, therefore, if a man is unable to work, but he is a faithful servant of God, he is saved and receives support from others. God giveth food to all flesh of his creation, every good and righteous blessing comes down from heaven from our loving and merciful living father who is our God. Supply all our needs upon this earth, according to all His riches in glory by Christ Jesus. It is God's good pleasure to give us good and perfect gifts; because God gave us everything on the earth; therefore, He owns everything. The salvation of man's souls comes from the divine command to work and support their divine family, which was instituted by our living Jehovah God.

Families are a divine institution, created, and instituted by our living Jehovah God at the very beginning of our time here on earth. God gave our father and our mother the ability to have children; therefore every child born upon the earth is a heritage of God, and He requires their spirit back upon the death of our body; because our spirit is in the express image of our living Jehovah God in heaven. God commanded our father and mother to be fruitful and have children to replenish the earth. Therefore, every child is given to the mother as a gift from our living Jehovah God. A child is a great blessing from God and they are to obey their parents and help work with the needs of their household. God gives every family upon the earth rain and dew from the heavens to sustain their lives. He also gave them all the seasons of the earth, He gave them springtime when the earth comes alive, and summertime to enjoy the fruits of the earth, and fall time for the harvesting of the fruits of the earth, and wintertime to prepare the earth with the waters of life of all the vegetation and fruits of the earth that comes in spring. The salvation of the mother's souls comes in preserving the divine institution of the family by having children.

One of Christian's greatest gifts from our Living God is that He hears and answers every prayer that we make. First, we must understand how it is that God can hear our every prayer, even the silent prayers. The Holy Spirit of God lives in the bodies of every Christian and our living God in heaven can communicate with His spirit that lives in our body. God's Spirit also helps us Christians with our physical and mental infirmities, and He makes intercession with God on our behalf, relaying all our prayers to God for us. God can hear His Spirit and God answers all our prayers according to His will. God treasures up all our prayers in heaven as a memorial to us Christians, because He loves us to rely on Him, putting our trust and confidence in Him. If we ask God for anything, He hears the prayers of the righteous, and if we have faith that we receive our request, and not doubt God, then He gives it to us. You know how you like to give good gifts to your children? Then you know that God gives you so much more good things, because it is His good pleasure to give them to you that ask of Him. If you want to know the power of prayer and very useful prayer to the Living God, read my book *The Lake of Fire Is Real and Here on Earth*. If you want to know the power of repentance of sins to God, then read my book *My Guardian Angel Visits* by Jerry Campbell.

Jehovah God gives His children when they decide to become a Christian a new heart. When we are born again of God, He gives us His Holy Spirit to live in our bodies, and this is the highest spiritual gift from God. The Spirit of God converts our former carnal mind into a spiritual mind that brings us Christian's eternal life and peace. The Holy Spirit is the spirit of God and Christ; He leads us Christians in the paths of righteousness here on earth. The Holy Spirit bears witness to God, that we are the children of God and heirs of God and Christ. The gifts of God that his spirit gives us are awesome, and the spirit will transform our character here on earth. We worship God in church every week, and we work in the Lord's vineyard in the church by going about the earth doing good unto all Mankind. Our minds are renewed in a mind of love for everyone, as the Spirit erases our minds of all hatred for other people. We obey the Laws of our land, and we become model citizens upon the earth; whereas, others can see the Spirit of God and Jesus living in our bodies. The spirit gives us Christians the divine wisdom and the power to understand the Holy Scriptures. Christians who keep the commandments of God written in the New Testament, having love, peace, and honor with integrity.

God gave us Christians the kingdom of God, which is the church that Jesus established on earth for Him. In this church, God had given us Christians a hundred times more earthly fathers, and mothers, and sisters and brothers than we had before we entered into the Kingdom of God. We become as one in our unity as brethren, and we are fellow workers together in the vineyard of the Lord. We are a Christian family caring for one another, like a literal family on earth who shares a love for one another and shares in the work of the Family. The preachers, elders, and deacons are like our literal fathers who rule over the flock of God in His church. They are to perfect the flock in the work of the ministry of building up the congregations. They are to bring every member of the flock into the unity of the faith, and knowledge about Jesus Christ until we become a perfect Christian likened unto the Lord Jesus Christ as our example to follow. Then we can build up the Kingdom of God with our love and our good works in the church.

Our living Jehovah God opens the windows of heaven and pours blessings upon the righteous Christians of the earth, for He loves to bless us. God blesses His people with strength and Peace. God blesses them that fear Him; all the poor and all the rich people of the earth. Jehovah God blesses the nation that serves Him, and He blesses all the people whom he has chosen to inherit the Kingdom of Heaven. Blessed are all who walk in the counsel of our living God and delights in the laws of our God, therein meditates in the Holy Bible day and night. Moreover, they reject all the counsel of the ungodly and does not run with the sinners of the earth, and He does not associate with the scornful ungodly of the earth. God makes them like a tree that is planted down on a riverbank, they enjoy the waters of life and bring forth good fruits and everything that they do in life, God prospers them. However, be not deceived, this is not so with the sinners and the ungodly of the earth, they cannot stand in the Day of Judgment, or in the congregation of the righteous in heaven. God sent Jesus Christ to earth to give all the people a great blessing in turning every one of us Christians away from our sins.

Moreover, Jesus promised Christians that it is more blessed to give than to receive.

Jehovah God said, "Blessed are the poor in spirit; for theirs is the Kingdom of Heaven."

We must go about the earth always being humble and kind to everyone, because God is not a respecter of persons, regarding their stature in this life on earth, nor does He regard any race or color of persons. Blessed are the meek: for they shall inherit the earth, being the New Earth that will descend from heaven, beginning at the end of this earth time. We must go about the earth being very patient and having a mild attitude toward all the people of the earth. We must be very slow to anger and not resentful toward other people. Blessed are the merciful; for they shall obtain mercy from God. We must go about the earth having compassion for other people and having forgiveness of their trespasses against us, having clemency toward others. Blessed are the pure in heart; for they shall see God in heaven. We must go about the earth, confessing our sins to God, praying for his forgiveness, and repenting of all our sins; thereby having a pure heart being free from sin. Blessed are the peacemakers; for they shall be called the children of God. We must go about the earth seeking peace, do not offend other people or quarrel with others. Remember that every idle word that mankind shall speak, we will have to give an account to Jesus Christ in our Day of Judgment, so be slow to speak and quick to hear others. We must not speak evil of others but must seek to settle quarrels among others, and we were the Children of God and fit for heaven. Blessed are they which are persecuted for righteousness' sake; for theirs is the Kingdom of Heaven. Many Christians in the Middle

East were persecuted for serving the Living God and Jesus Christ by the terrorist. They were murdered because of their faith and the terrorist executed them on American TV, yet the Christians would not deny their faith in the Lord, but our living Jehovah God said, "Great would be their reward in heaven; for so did the ungodly persecute unto their death the prophets and apostles which was before them."

We must go about the Earth standing up for our faith in our living God, even until our death, for God has said, "Be you faithful until death and I will give you a crown of life."

There are many rewards that our living Jehovah God gives us while we are here on earth. God said for Christians to love our enemies and do good unto them, and lend, hoping for nothing back in return. And your reward shall be great, and you shall be the children of the highest God; for He is kind to the unthankful and the evil. When Christians does good works to others on earth, our reward from God is glory, honor, and peace. God said in the Kingdom of Heaven it will be like a man on earth who traveled to a faraway country, before he went, he called all his servants together and he gave them his goods according to their abilities; and to one servant, he gave five talents, to another he gave two talents, and to another he gave one talent, and immediately he went on his journey. Then after a long time, the lord of those servants came and settled with them the accounts and the servant that received five talents and two talents went and traded with them and increased his talents double and when they told the lord the good news, the lord said, "Well, done you good and faithful servant, you were faithful over a few things, I will make you ruler over many things. Enter into the joys of the lord," but the servant of the lord that had one-talent ability was given one talent. And he was afraid to trade the talent, so he went and hid the talent in the ground and when his lord returned, he gave the lord back his talent and his lord said, "You wicked and lazy servant, so you should have deposited my money with the bankers and when I returned, you would have had my money plus interest. So cast the unprofitable servant into outer darkness where there will be weeping and gnashing of teeth."

God gives us Christians power over evil, today Satan only has the power over us that we give Him. The Christians that convert people to serve righteousness on the earth will shine in heaven like the stars forever and ever.

The key of wisdom to understanding the living Jehovah God has left to His church that His son, Jesus Christ, came to earth and established. God entrusted the manifold wisdom of God to the church, and He made the church leaders the custodians of His wisdom. They must handle the oracles, which are the words of God precisely as God spoke them to mankind as recorded in the Holy Bible. Humanity can only obtain this wisdom of God by being born again, begotten by the oracles of God, and worship God in His church, keeping His commandments. Therefore, you can have true wisdom, which you can obtain eternal life in heaven, but the wisdom of the world is just foolishness with God.

Chapter Twenty
The Righteous Living in Mansions Made with Gold, Pearl, and Precious Stones

Jehovah God has already prepared the New Heaven, and there are many mansions for the saved people of the earth to live in when they go to heaven. Apostle John saw the New Heaven coming down out of heaven from God and John compared the beauty of the city of god as likened unto a bride of the earth that is adorned beautifully for her new husband. The City of God in heaven equally built-in breadth, height, and length, totaling 1380 miles. The name of the city is New Jerusalem and is patterned after the walled city of Jerusalem in Israel back in the days when Solomon was the King of Israel. Apostle John saw this City of God in a vision, and it had a high and high wall around the city, and there were twelve gates in the wall with twelve angels guarding the gates. There were three gates on each side of the city; three on the north, south, west, and east side of the city with the names of the twelve tribes of Israel written on the gates. Moreover, the wall of the city had twelve foundations, with the names of the twelve apostles of Jesus written on them. The twelve gates made out of pearl and the gates of the city will never close. There is no night in heaven, just day. Also, the twelve foundations weremade out of the most precious stones known to God. The construction of the city was made of pure gold and it was as clear as transparent glass. Apostle John did not see any temple in the city, because Jehovah God and Jesus Christ are the light of the city. The nations of the saved walk in the city and the kings and rulers of the earth bring glory to the city. The citizens of the city of God, or the New Heaven or New Earth; live forever and ever with Jehovah God and Jesus Christ.

The citizens of the Kingdom of Heaven; they rest from their labors, because God furnishes all their needs, they never hunger or thirst again. The sun shall not shine upon them or any heat; because Jesus Christ who sits in the midst of the throne is their shepherd and He leads them to living fountains of water, and God shall wipe away every tear from their eyes, there is no weeping. God has mansions in the City of God, made of pure gold as clear as crystal glass, and God has priceless treasures and rewards in store for all the citizens of the Kingdom of Heaven. All the citizens of the Kingdom of Heaven is made equal to the holy angels who are in heaven. There are not any marriages in heaven; we all live together in peace, love, and friendship. Moreover, all the saved people can live in the New Earth and New Heaven; being equal to angels, we can travel from one to the other in a matter of an instant.

Apostle John saw the New Heaven and New Earth; for the first heaven and first earth had passed away and the earth did not have any seas. Jesus Christ came down from heaven, and he testified to everything written in the Holy Bible. There were about five hundred Christians and all the apostles witnessed Jesus Christ going back to heaven in the clouds of glory with many holy angels from heaven, whom God sent for Jesus. When the Pharisees stoned the Christian Stephen to death, just before he was stoned, God showed Stephen in a vision; when he looked into the heavens, God opened up the heavens, and he saw God and Jesus standing at the right-hand side of God in heaven. Apostle Paul was preaching Jesus Christ to the people of Iconium who worshipped idols, they took Paul outside the city limits and stoned him to death. Flesh and blood body cannot enter into heaven, but his spirit departed out of his body, and God called him into the third heavens of paradise. There, Apostle Paul witnessed seeing a man there he knew was in the Lord, thirteen years earlier here on earth. In paradise, Paul saw Jesus Christ there, and he begged Jesus to remove the throne in his flesh that Satan buffeted him with, but the lord told Paul that His Grace was sufficient for him.

One day, a man came into our Dollar Store wearing a tee shirt which read John 10:10, "I said, so you are a man of God, and he said, 'Yes. Let me tell you why I know that you think there are beautiful places on this earth, but I tell you that heaven makes this earth look like a dump.' I said, 'How do you know?'"

He said, "When he was ten years old, his parents gave him to his uncle to raise, and his uncle was an evil man. One day, he got mad at him, and he hung him with his belt on the front porch until he died. He testified that his spirit went to heaven and he saw the most beautiful wonders of heaven than I could imagine."

I said, "Well, how did you come back to earth?"

He said, "There was a nurse who lived just up the road, and she had to walk past our house, and she saw me hanging, and my face was black as coal, and he was a white man."

The nurse cut him down and revived him with CPR. Also, brought him to life again, so his spirit returned to his body.

Jesus said in John 10:10, *"The thief came to steal, and kill and destroy. I came that my followers (sheep) might have life and have it more abundantly."*

It is true of all people upon the earth today, those who are Christian's blessed above measure and those who are sinners and ungodly, they come upon others to steal, kill, or destroy everything they can on this earth.

The keys of wisdom of understanding how beautiful heaven must be and how the saved who are the heirs of the Kingdom of Heaven is written in the Holy Bible. All who go to heaven are known in heaven as you are known on earth today. However, if you die from Injuries on earth, in heaven you have a perfect body like the angels of heaven have. If you die on earth from any disease, in heaven, your body is free from all sickness, and you have a perfect body. If you die on earth from any mental disease, in heaven, your mind is perfect, as well as your body. When saved on earth and you lose your mind, when you die, you are saved and go to heaven. If you go to heaven, you remember your life on earth, as well as the people you once knew on earth. In heaven, you know all the people that you knew on earth who are saved and now live in the New Heaven and New Earth.

Chapter Twenty-One

The Eternal Punishment of All Sinners and Ungodly in the Lake of Fire

The earth that we live on today is reserved by Jehovah God to become the place of the eternal lake of fire. Moreover, become the eternal home of all the sinners that can't cease from their sins and all the ungodly that have rejected the counsel of Jehovah God. Moreover, all the lost souls from the beginning of earth time until the end of earth time, which now live in hell, they are in reserve in hell until the end of time, then God transfers them to the lake of fire which is this present earth.

The last day of earth time comes like any other day you have experienced during your lifetime and it is the day on one side of the earth and is the night on the other side of the earth. People will be going about their daily business, as usual, they will be shocked when they realize this is their judgment day. When they see Jesus Christ, whom the people of his time on earth have portrayed his image in pictures of him, but in that day, when the Lord Jesus Christ descends from heaven, sitting upon his great white judgment throne, every eye that is upon the earth at that time will look up into the heavens above and they will see Jesus coming. And Jesus will have about forty thousand holy angels of God coming with him, and they will go to the four corners of the earth and gather up all the people that are lost. The holy angels will gather up the saved and sit them on the right-hand side of the great white judgment throne of Jesus and they will sit the lost on the left-hand side of the great white throne of Jesus.

This last day of time will come just like a thief in the night, unexpected and suddenly to all the people of the earth that are sinners and ungodly. There will be two people working in the field and one will be taken by the angels and one will be left in the field. There will be many working in factories and few will be taken and many will be left. There will be many at ball games and few will be taken and many will be left. There will be nations of people and the holy angels of God will take a few and they will leave many. Why will the angels do this? Well, judgment first must begin at the house of Jehovah God and all those that the angels of God take first are the saved people of the Kingdom of Heaven; their names are written in The Book of Life that God will send with Jesus to the Judgment. And all the people whose names are written in the book of life have already been judged by Jehovah God in heaven.

When Jesus descends from heaven for Judgment Day, he will bring with him all the saved souls that have died and are awaiting this day, living in paradise. When the Lord descends from Heaven, the Arch Angel will give a big shout and blow the trumpet of God, then Jesus will give a shout and all the saved in the graves will hear his voice, and all the dead in Christ are raised first. The saved from paradise will be joined up with their bodies that were raised from the graves. And these bodies will be celestial bodies which are their heavenly bodies, equal to the angels in heaven. All the saved people have already been judged by God and Jesus Christ in heaven and written them in the book of life. Jesus will change all the bodies of everyone living on earth at his coming, in a twinkling of an eye, from a terrestrial body to a celestial body that never dies, regardless where Jesus Christ judges you to spend an eternity in heaven or The Lake of Fire. Now Jesus Christ will deliver all the saved souls back to his father in heaven at this time because they are prejudged by Jesus and God every day they have lived on earth. Jesus will say unto them, "Well done, you good and faithful servants. Enter you into the joys of the Lord."

Now comes the judgment of all the sinners who many thought they were saved, but they could not cease from their sinning and they would not repent of their sins. Now Jesus will start the judgment of all the sinners who have gone to church every Sunday, but they have committed sins they refuse to repent of them or they have failed to keep the commandments of Jesus Christ as written in the New Covenant. Today, on Judgment Day, they will be very disappointed and many will say to Jesus, "Lord, Lord, have we not prophesied in your name and in your name cast out devils and, in your name, done many wonderful works?"

Then Jesus will tell them, "I never knew you. Depart from me, you that worked sins." Jesus said, "As I see and hear, I judge people every minute of every day they lived upon the earth."

How can Jesus know every word and ever works that every one of us People on Earth does? Well, when Jesus went back to heaven, he sent the Holy Spirit of God down to earth on a mission. The Holy Spirit lives in the bodies of Christian's and God and Jesus who live in heaven, they know what is in the mind of the Holy Spirit who will testify to them our every word and deed that we do. The Holy Spirit will testify to Jesus and God of the sins that people commit, and He will testify of the righteous deeds that people do on earth, and He will testify to Jesus of these things on our judgment day.

When Jesus judges the world at the last day of earth time, he will bring with him from heaven all the books that he will use to judge people from. The people before God sent Jesus to earth to make a new covenant with; Jesus will have all the books of the Old Covenant to judge them from. Jesus will have all the books of the New Covenant to judge all the people from since he arose from the dead and ascended back to heaven to his father and his throne. Jesus will have with him the Book of Life that God and Jesus write all the names of the saved people at his coming back for the last judgment day. Now all the lost people will stand before Jesus Christ, regardless of their status in their life on earth, from the small to the greatest of them. Now all that are in their graves and in hell will stand before Jesus, and be judged according to their works and death and hell were cast into the Lake of Fire.

Where is the Lake of Fire? You are standing upon the very place that God has reserved back for this day; it is the earth now. What will God do now after Jesus has judged all the sinner's and ungodly and passed his judgment upon every one of them? Well, all the planets and all the stars will pass away with a great noise as they crash into the abyss. All these planets in our solar system will all be dissolved by being burned up. Now Jesus will do the same thing to earth that he did to Sodom and Gomorrah when he judged them guilty of grievous sins. The same day that Jesus went out of Sodom back into heaven, he rained out of heaven's fire and brimstones and destroyed them all. And now Jesus has completed the judgment, he will do the same to earth; he will rain down upon the earth fire and brimstones out of heaven and turn the entire earth into a Lake of Fire and all the elements of the earth will melt with the fevering heat, all the buildings upon the earth will melt in these flames, all the air that we enjoy today on earth will all burn up with this fire, all the water in the seas, lakes, rivers, and streams upon the earth will be all burned up by this fire. All the trees and vegetation will all be burned up. When the sun and moon, along with all the planets and stars crash and burn, it will be total darkness above the flames of the Lake of Fire.

Now I will testify to you and before everyone in heaven and on earth how I know all these things about the Lake of Fire. My mother was a good Christian woman who went to church every Sunday and she sits me down about the age of five and six, she taught me everything in the Scriptures about hell. It came to pass when I was seven years old. I came down sick with chicken pox, measles, and mumps with a temperature of about one hundred and six. First, I got sick with chicken pox, the next day, I came down with the measles on top of the chicken pox, and on the third day, I came down sick with the mumps and the high temperature. My body was entirely covered with chicken pox and measles; they made my body stink really bad. My parents had ten children and they couldn't afford to take me to the doctor. This happened in the winter of nineteen and fifty and the winters in the mountains of Eastern Kentucky was very cold, with snows from twelve to twenty-four inches high in those days.

On the third day, my father came to my bed early in the morning and wanted to buy me something at the little country store at the mouth of Browns Fork Kentucky and deliver it to me between his coal hauls. He always got up before his children and come in after we were in bed because he hauled coal for a living. Well, I was surprised that he would do this for me, but I said, "Daddy, I don't want you to have to do this for me, because you work so hard raising all us children and I am not that sick."

He was persistent and said, "Do you want a candy bar or a small cup of ice cream?"

I saw he was determined to buy me something, so I said, "No, daddy, I want you to buy me a whole box of ice-cream."

When he delivered me the ice-cream, my throat was so swollen that I could not swallow the first bite. That night on the third day, all our family, except Daddy, was sitting around the coal fireplace in a circle, sitting in ladder back chairs that salesmen came around selling door to door. Behind the fireplace was my mother's bed where she slept by herself; Daddy slept in the other bedroom, and beside her bed is where I and my two brothers slept. The later in the night it got, the worse I felt, so I said to Mother, "I am going to have to get in bed, I am feeling very sick," and she said,

"Jerry, tonight you get to sleep in any bed in this house you want to, tonight."

I said, "You are kidding," and she said, "No, I am not, do you want to sleep in my bed?" and I said, "Yes."

The longer I lay there, the sicker I became, and it occurred to me that I would die this night. I was chilling to death and begging Mother for more covers until I got all the covers except one for each bed in the house that night. When I thought about dying and being in the grave, that it was the end of my life with my family, and I would never see them again. So I thought that I better get a good look at my family, because I would not see them again. When I pulled the covers down, looking at the backs of their head, I heard Mother crying and scolding the rest of the children, saying, "You all better shut up," crying and saying Daddy loves Jerry more than them, because this is the first time we ever had ice-cream in this house. Boyd, who is my father, she said was upset, because if we had the money, we could take Jerry to Hazard to the doctor and save him, "We don't expect him to make it through the night."

So I pulled the covers up over my head and I really began to cry rivers of tears, thinking how sad to die so young.

I thought, *Shall I tell Mother that I heard her*? and I thought, *Why? Because they can't save me, how sad to be so poor and no one this earth can save me!*

As I laid there crying, it occurred to me, I know somebody that can save me, God can. He made the heavens and the earth and everything in them, He made me and He can save me! Mommy has been teaching me about God and I believed in Him and I loved Him because He took the poor bum Lazarus to heaven and threw the rich man in hell. And I was so poor like Lazarus was, we didn't have anything. My mother would let all her children eat supper at night and she would wait until we eat, then she would eat the scraps left over and she always prayed to God and thank Him for the scraps in the name of Jesus, and I would think, *If that is all I got for supper, I would not bless them in the name of Jesus*, but Jesus must have thought, *Yes, you will.*

Well I had to have an answer from God that night or I would not live to see tomorrow, I was at the end of my rope, and no one on the earth could save me, but God could. So I prayed to God, twice and did not ask in the name of Jesus, never got my answer. I had never prayed to God at this age, so I thought, *I will pray one more time and I am going to do like Mommy does; ask God in the name of Jesus.* And I am going to make a deal with God, if He will heal me and let me live to be an old man, that I would do something for Him that He would be very proud of me for doing, I didn't know what; but I would do something. I didn't think that I could be a good teenager and repay God, because I was playing with a little girl and thought to have sex with her, but I didn't. I knew I had to be honest with God because He knew everything. This is why I thought that I could not be a good teenager, because of my sexual desires.

My third prayer to God, with tears running down my face like rivers, I prayed my silent prayer to God on this wise, "Dear God, I am so sick, I will not make it through tonight, there is no one upon the earth that can save me. I am too young to die and I don't want to die, I want to live to be an old man. I want to make a deal with you; if You will heal me and let me live to be an old man when I become

145

an old man, I will do something that you will be very proud of me for doing, I don't know what; but I will do something. I would promise you that I would do something for you as a teenager, but I don't think that I can be a good teenager. I have to be honest with you, because I believe that if you accept my deal, you know all the days of my life. I was playing with this little girl and I had an evil thought to have sex with her, but I didn't. If you don't heal me and I die tonight, You have to bring me to heaven, because I have not committed any sins. But why do that? Please heal me, I want to live. Now please answer me in the name of Jesus Christ."

I laid there for about a minute or two, no answer came, so I said, "God, I know you are there and you don't have to answer me, but my mother has been reading me the Bible and I believe in you and I love you because you took the bum Lazarus to heaven and threw the rich man into hell and I am poor like Lazarus, we don't have nothing. You don't have to answer me."

Well, God answered my prayers in about one minute and I could tell that I got to God's heart with my crying prayers. He said in a voice of an old man, in a little grievous voice, "Little boy, why are you crying? Look again, these same people that you see tonight, when you awaken tomorrow, you will see again. Now lay down and go to sleep."

This startled me and I thought, *I better do just like He told me to do*, so I pulled the covers down and looked at my family around the fireplace and pulled the covers back over my head and went into a deep sleep.

That night God took my spirit, high above my home and encased my spirit in a crystal clear case, that shielded me

146

from the flames, and He showed me the actual Lake of Fire, in a 20/20 vision, as clear as day, that will come upon the earth on the last day of time. The flames were approximately 100 feet high, and the whole earth as far as my eyes could see was burning with these flames of fire. The location of my home that I was raised up is located on Highway 456 at the mouth of Browns Fork Holler. Our home sits in the seven-acre field, as you turn to go up the holler, on the right-hand side. There are mountains on each side of the seven-acre field that we planted every year and the field sits down in the valley between the mountains. This is what the Lake of Fire looks like; the flames were the strangest fire I ever saw on earth; they were a creamy white color with yellow color at the ends of the flames. The whole earth looked like a pure Lake of Fire and there was black smoke ascending off the flames into the heavens. Then I looked into the heavens and it was silky black from the smoke and darkness, because I did not see the sun, moon, or any stars in the heavens, they were all gone. This scared me and I began to cry, saying, "I thought that God took my deal," but He has let me die and go to hell and it felt as someone shook me. Then I heard two women talking to each other about the middle of the seven-acre field that we planted every year.

One woman said to the other woman, "I don't know why God put me in here? I was a good woman all my life, I never did anything really bad, but I never served God."

While she was talking, I felt sorry for her, but afterward, I said to myself, "It is no wonder why God put you in here."

My mother goes to church every Sunday and serves God. Then the other woman said, "Well, I am like you, but before God done this to earth, I had plenty of wealth and I am so hot and miserable in these flames, I would give everything that I had for one glass of water."

As I looked over the Lake of Fire, I saw that the creek where I lived was burned up from the fire, I did not see any trees or vegetation, nor any living animals or birds, there was nothing, except the flames of fire upon the earth and nothing in the skies, except pure darkness.

Now I slept the entire night and this is all that I saw and heard until the next morning when I awakened. I threw the covers back and my entire bed was wet from sweating, and there was not a trace of the chicken pox, measles, or mumps, they were all gone completely from my body. The day was like God had promised me, I did see every one of my family that day before I went to bed that night. My box of ice-cream was eaten by my brother, but God has given me truckloads of ice-cream all the days of my life since then.

Now I am an old man and I am serving My God Jehovah, to make Him very proud of me for being one of his many servants. Jehovah God is not willing that you should perish in the Lake of Fire, but He wishes that you would come to repentance of your sins and avoid this terrible place. You should not fear them that can kill your body, but cannot kill your spirit, but you should fear the living Jehovah God who has the power to destroy both your body and soul in the Lake of Fire for eternity. Be not deceived if God did not spare the angel's in heaven that rebelled against Him; but cast them into hell. And God did not spare the old world that sinned, saving Noah and his family only; God made it rain for forty days and nights and flooded the entire earth with water and destroyed them all.

And God did not save the cities of Sodom and Gomorrah; but He rained down fire and brimstone from heaven and destroyed them all, except Lot, who was a righteous man. Jesus warns the sinner's and ungodly that if your hand offends you by committing sins, you are better off if you cut your hand off than be cast into hell where the fire is never quenched. If your foot offends you, cut them off, it is more profitable to you in life than to be cast into hell. If your eye offends you, gouge them out, it would be better for you to enter into life with no eyes than to be cast into hell fire, where you never die and the fire is never quenched.

If you decide not to obey your living Jehovah God and lose your soul in The Lake of Fire, that will be right here on this earth. You will be walking through the earth naked, and your fellow citizens will be all the sinners and all the ungodly people who ever lived upon the earth, from the beginning of time to the end of time. Your neighbor will be the terrorist of this world, the drug dealer's and all drug heads and drunkards, all murders, homosexuals and lesbians, worshippers of false gods, false prophets, and preachers, with all people who are full of wickedness, covetousness, maliciousness, envy, debaters, deceitfulness, whisperers, backbiters, despiteful, haters of God, inventors of all evil things, disobedient to parents, lawbreakers, disrespectful, dis-honorable, without love in their hearts, without any self-control over their actions, they are unmerciful to others, rapists, robbers, thieves, and all manner of evil profane people as your fellow citizens.

The key of wisdom to understanding what eternal life will be like for you living in the Lake of Fire. Just think how hot a regular fire is and think that The Lake of Fire will burn eight times hotter than a regular fire burns. The sun is a planet that burns with fire and brimstones and it lights up the entire earth by day because the sun is the ruler of the day. God could use the sun to crash into the earth at the end of earth time and he already has the lake of fire in store for the last day of time. There must come a separation of the good people from the evil people at the end of time; otherwise, heaven would be just like earth is today.

Chapter Twenty-Two
The Holy Spirit Is the Power
of Jehovah God

The holy spirit of God is also called the Holy Ghost and He wears many different hats in the Godhead. There is just one Holy Spirit in the Godhead and He is the Spirit of God and Christ. The Holy Spirit is omnipotent, having unlimited power and authority. The Holy Spirit is the power source of God and Christ. Jesus, who was a spirit in heaven, was brought to earth by the power of the holy spirit of God. The Holy Spirit through the operation of the incarnation of Jesus into the body of a virgin named Mary prepared Jesus Christ with an earthly body. The Holy Spirit when Jesus was baptized, he descended from heaven in the bodily form of a dove and he came and entered into the body of Jesus. Therefore, Jesus had the full power of Jehovah God living inside his body all during his time he was here on earth. God gave Jesus all the words of the gospels through the Holy Spirit and this is how that when Jesus said, "The words that I speak are the words of my father and they are not the words of my own."

And again, Jesus said, "The words that I speak to you, they are Spirit and they are life, because the spirit of God lived in Him."

When they crucified Jesus and He lay in the grave dead, it was the holy spirit of God that raised Jesus from the dead. And if Christians die being in the Lord Jesus, the Holy Spirit of God will also make alive our mortal bodies by the spirit that lives in us.

The Holy Spirit of God and Christ is omnipresent, and He has the power to be in all places at the same time. The Prophet and King David said, "Where can I flee from your spirit? If I ascend up into heaven, He is there and if I descend down into hell, He is there also."

The Holy Spirit is given to every single Christian that is baptized and He lives in our bodies as our witness to God. Christians must first be born again of water baptism and of the spirit of God to enter into the Kingdom of God, which is the church that Jesus built here on earth. The spirit has no flesh and no bones like humans have, therefore, he can live inside the Christian bodies. There are about two billion Christians worldwide and He lives in every one of them all the time. He transmitted our prayers to God, even our silent prayers which are not spoken.

The Holy Spirit is omniscient, having the power to know all things that ever was, and now is and all things that are to come in the future. God has revealed all things to the apostles by His spirit; for the spirit searches all things of Jehovah God, even the deep things. Just as no man knows the things of a man, except the man's spirit that lives in him, even so the things of God knoweth no man, except the spirit of God. This is how that God who lives in heaven, knows our every thought and intent of our hearts. God knows our every word spoken and every work that we do upon the earth by the witness of His holy spirit that lives in our body. God has given His son, Jesus Christ, to have power over the Holy Spirit also, and this is how that when two or three people are gathered together in his name, he is in their midst. this is how Jesus who lives in heaven with God can say, as I hear and see, I judge and this would be every minute of every day and night we have on earth. This is how God and Christ keep the books in heaven of our sins and whose name goes into their Book of Life or is to be taken out of the Book of Life.

The Holy Spirit is the workhorse of the Godhead; because He is the power of the highest God. The Holy Spirit at the beginning of earth time; when the earth was without form and covered the entire earth. The Holy Spirit moved upon the face of the waters in the darkness. Whatever God commanded, the Holy Spirit did the work in the creation. This is why Jesus commanded that we are baptized into all three members that make up the Godhead. He is a witness to everything that goes on upon the earth and He will testify and bear our record to God and Christ all the works that we have done on earth.

The Kingdom of Heaven is a kingdom made up of spirits, God, Christ, and the Holy Spirit are all spirits in heaven, so are all the holy angels in heaven. Now when we die and go to heaven, we, too, will all be spirits, equal to the holy angels in heaven.

The Holy Spirit is responsible for all the Holy Scriptures from the beginning to the end. God sent the Holy Spirit to live in all the prophets of the Old Testament and they spoke the words that God instructed the Holy Spirit to inspire them to write. Jesus said the Spirit makes alive and the words that he spoke to the disciples were spirit and life. The Holy Ghost by the mouth of the Prophet David spoke concerning Judas, which was a guide to them that took Jesus and crucified Him. Apostle Paul said that the Holy Spirit spoke expressly through Him, saying that in the latter days of time, some shall depart from the faith, giving heed to seducing spirits and doctrines of devils. The Holy Spirit of God lived in all the prophets, Jesus, and all the apostles and delivered God's words through them.

The key of wisdom to understanding the Holy Spirit of God and Christ is to understand that just as you have a spirit that returns to God who gave it to you after your death, to be judged and put in paradise or hell for eternity. We have one God, one lord, one spirit, one church, one faith, one baptism, one hope of our calling, one God and father who is through all and lives in you all. Just as the Holy Scriptures are not God, not Jesus Christ, and not the Holy Spirit, but the scriptures are their work. All the scripture are the oracles of Jehovah God. And God, Christ, and the Holy Spirit are all referred to as, being a He, which makes Him a male spirit person.

Chapter Twenty-Three

The Holy Spirit Lives in Christians and Helps Them with Their Lives

Christian's Bodies are the temple of Jehovah God and the Spirit of God lives in us and if anyone defiles the temple of God by committing sins, God will destroy us, because the temple of God is holy, as we are holy. Christians are warned against apostasy by leaving the principles of the doctrine of Christ as taught us in the New Testament. For it is impossible for all those who have been enlightened by the words of the Holy Bible and have tasted of the heavenly gift, and were made partakers of the Holy Ghost, and have tasted of the good word of God, and the powers of the world to come. If they shall fall away by the desertion of our faith and false doctrines, to renew them again unto repentance, seeing how they have crucified the son of God again and put Him to an open shame.

When Jesus ascended back to heaven, he told his apostles to wait in Jerusalem and they shall be baptized with the Holy Ghost on the day of Pentecost, which is 50 days from the ascension. Now on the 50th, the day the Holy

Ghost descended from heaven, like a mighty rushing wind, in the form of split tongues of fire that came and sat upon each of the apostles and they were baptized with the Holy Ghost. And He gave them the power to speak in tongues of every nation as the Spirit gave them utterance to speak. This confounded the people, how could people from every nation understand Peter in their own language? The Holy Ghost gave them the power to be a witness for Jesus Christ in Jerusalem and the whole world. People came from every nation under the heavens to see and hear the apostles speak in split tongues and Apostle Peter stood up and delivered a powerful sermon. Then about three thousand believed and said, "Men and brethren, what must we do to be saved?" and Apostle Peter said, "Repent and be baptized every one of you in the name of Jesus Christ for the remission of sins and you shall receive the gift of the Holy Ghost."

This is the condition for people who believe in Jesus to receive the Holy Spirit to live in our bodies. Now this is what Jesus meant when he said to Nicodemus, "Except a man be born again of water and of the spirit, he cannot enter into the Kingdom of God, which is the church that Jesus built."

Jesus gave Apostle Peter the keys to the Kingdom of God and he used those keys on the day of Pentecost to open up the doors to the Kingdom of God. This is the condition that Jehovah God put on mankind that makes us qualified to receive the gift of the Holy Ghost, which is His spirit.

When Christians have the Holy Spirit living in them, they are begotten by Jesus Christ, and they no longer walk after the flesh; but we walk after the Spirit of God that lives in our bodies. The law of the Spirit of God and Christ is eternal life and sets us free from the law of sin and death. If us Christians walk our whole lives serving God and Christ, the Holy Spirit lives in us and this same spirit raised up Jesus from the dead. If he dwells in our bodies when we die, he will also make alive our mortal bodies at the last day of time at the resurrection. The Holy Spirit makes Christian's spiritual, whereas we can understand the scriptures, comparing spiritual things with spiritual things, but the natural person can't understand the scriptures, they are foolishness to him, they are spiritually discerned. The Holy Spirit teaches us the Scriptures; He is the spirit of understanding and the spirit of wisdom to all faithful Christians. He is the spirit of holiness, goodness, and he gives us Christian's hope, comfort, peace, and joy when we remain obedient to God. For as many as are led by the spirit of God, they are the sons of God. The Holy Spirit of God beareth witness with our spirit to God that we are indeed the children of God and this qualifies us to inherit the Kingdom of Heaven. The Holy Spirit that lives in Christian's bodies, He helps us with our physical and moral weaknesses in our prayers to Jehovah God. We don't always know what we should pray for, but the Holy Spirit does and He makes intercessions for us to God with groanings that cannot be spoken or heard by Humans. Jehovah God knows what is in the minds of all Christians, as well as what is in the mind of the Holy Spirit; because He makes prayers to God for us Christian's. This is how God can hear our silent prayers that we make to him.

Whosoever believes that Jesus is the Christ is born of God and everyone who loves the brethren and loves Jehovah God is born of God. This is how we Christians know that we are children of God when we love Him and keep His commandments, and they are not grievous. Christians, who are born of God, can overcome the world of sin, just as the Lord Jesus has done when he lived on earth. There are three that bear witness in the earth, the holy Spirit, the water baptism, and the blood of Christ shed on the Cross. And there are three witnesses in heaven, the father of everything in heaven and on earth, the word which is God's son, Jesus Christ, and Jehovah God and Jesus Christ, Holy Spirit, and these three are one. The Holy Spirit bears witness to God in heaven of all mankind, because the spirit is the truth.

The key of wisdom to understanding the Holy Spirit of Jehovah God and Jesus Christ is to know that He is a spirit, which does not have flesh and bones like mankind has. This makes Him likened to our spirit that comes forth upon our death and goes before Jesus for the judgment. This spirit of mankind is invisible and so is the Holy Spirit of God. The Holy Spirit is the workhorse of the Godhead, God and Christ tell the Holy Spirit what they want and he does the work for them. He did the work in the creation, He gave Moses and all the prophets, the old scriptures and He gave Jesus and His apostles all the scriptures of the New Testament. The Holy Spirit lives in all Christian's and he is our witness to God and Christ and he will justify or condemn us before them in heaven. The Holy Spirit is the third person in the Godhead.

Chapter Twenty-Four
The Holy Spirit a Witness to All Mankind's Lives

The Holy Spirit of God and Christ has important work today here on earth that is a matter of eternal life or eternal death to all people. When God brought Jesus back to heaven, He sent the Holy Spirit down from heaven to finish out the work of God until the end of earth time. One of His missions is to reprove the sinners and the ungodly people of their sin are to God. The Holy Spirit will keep God informed of all their sins. The Holy Spirit will not live in the bodies of the sinners and the ungodly people of the world. But He will observe every word and every deed that every sinner and ungodly persons commit upon the earth. And He will reprove them to God.

Another work of the Holy Spirit on earth today is He will live in the Christian's bodies to help them with their lives, because they are servants of Jehovah God. The Holy Spirit will testify to God of every word and every deed that we Christians do upon the earth. This is how God and Christ know them that belong to them on earth. The Holy Spirit relays our prayers to God in heaven and God saves all our prayers for a memorial to every Christian on earth. God loves our prayers and He answers every one of them according to his will and not according to our will. The Holy Spirit is the truth, He guides us Christians in the paths of righteousness, He leads into all truths, He gives us wisdom, love, peace, joy, longsuffering, gentleness, goodness, faith, meekness, temperance, against such things as these, there is no law against them. When we Christian's do these things, other people know that we have the spirit of God and Christ living in our bodies.

Another great work of the Holy Spirit of God and Christ on earth today is He will reprove every person that ever lived upon the earth in their judgment to God and Christ. The Holy Spirit is their witness upon the earth of every person who ever lived on earth. When we die and our spirit comes forth and goes before Jesus Christ to be judged, the Holy Spirit will testify of our works that we have done while we lived here on Earth. He will justify the faithful Christians, and He will condemn the sinners that didn't quit their sinning and the ungodly at their judgment. Satan and his angels have already been judged and sent to hell, to await the end of time Judgment Day, and then they will be cast into the Lake of Fire, which is going to be here on this present earth. Now all the sinners and ungodly people of the earth today have the spirit of Satan living in their bodies. And they are those who walk in disobedience to Jehovah God. All the people of the world that did not believe in Jesus Christ will be lost at their judgment.

The Holy Spirit is a guide and Jesus Christ sent him to live in every apostle, to help them remember what Jesus told them while he was with them. And He would guide them into all truth because He would not speak of Himself; but whatsoever that Jesus told Him to speak, that is what the apostles would hear from the spirit. The Holy Spirit would glorify Jesus Christ as He would hear what Jesus wanted him to tell the apostles and He would show them things to come in the future.

The Holy Spirit is the comforter to the apostles and to all Christians today and He will be living in all Christian's bodies forever on earth and in heaven. The comforter is the Holy Ghost, whom the Father will send to earth in Jesus' name and He will bring all things to the apostle's remembrance that Jesus taught them while on earth with them. The Holy Spirit will comfort all Christians today unto all that mourn; God is a God of Comfort to all that love and obeys Him.

Christians are saved by the washing of regeneration and renewing of the Holy Ghost. Jesus Christ told Nicodemus that except a man be born again, he cannot see the Kingdom of God which is the church. Jesus said that we must be born again of water and of the spirit or we cannot enter into the Kingdom of God. When Christians are baptized, God gives us His Holy Spirit to live in our bodies to regenerate us from a sinful nature and transform us into a spiritual nature. When Jehovah God made mankind, who was Adam and his wife, Eve, they were perfect in their righteousness to God. When we are baptized for the forgiveness of our sins, we receive the Gift from Jehovah God, His Holy Spirit for the purpose of being spiritually reborn that causes us to be completely reformed and improved. This is the work of the Holy Spirit to regenerate the children of God, preparing us for the Kingdom of Heaven. The Holy Spirit leads us into the paths of righteousness.

The key of wisdom to understanding the holy spirit of God is to believe in God with all your heart, soul, and mind, likewise have the same faith in His son, Jesus Christ. If you have faith, without doubting their words in the Scriptures and obey the commands, you will come to understand all these things written in the Scriptures. You will take heed to God's commandments when He said, "Grieve not the Holy Spirit of God because the Holy Spirit seals your fate unto the day of your judgment."

Again, God warns us not to quench the Holy Spirit, not to extinguish Him by putting Him out of your life by your unbelief in Him. Do not be likened unto the Pharisees and Sadducees who always resisted the Holy Spirit of God by not accepting the Scriptures that taught them about the Holy Spirit. As a result, the Holy Ghost would not live in their bodies because he was not welcome and they became very evil and their works were wicked.

Chapter Twenty-Five
The Unforgivable Sin Against the Holy Spirit

How can people commit the sin unto their death, which is the blasphemy against the Holy Ghost? Here is one example, One Sabbath day, Jesus went into the temple and when he was leaving the temple, the rulers of the Pharisees took counsel against Jesus, seeking how they could destroy him. When Jesus was leaving Jerusalem, the people brought a man to Jesus that was possessed with a devil, that had struck this man blind and dumb and Jesus healed him and He both received his sight and He spoke again. And when the evil Pharisees saw what Jesus did, they accused Jesus of casting out the devil by the power of Satan. Now these Pharisees committed blasphemy against the Holy Ghost by speaking evil against Him. Because it was by the power of God's Holy Ghost that Jesus cast out the devil and healed this man and not by the power of Satan. Jesus told the Pharisees what sin they just committed. He said all manner of sins and blasphemies shall be forgiven by mankind, except the blasphemy against the Holy Ghost shall never be forgiven unto mankind in this world or in the world to come.

Today, there is a way that any Christian can commit the sin of blasphemy against the Holy Ghost, which is the unforgivable sin unto death when any Christian leaves the commandments that God gave mankind in the New Testament covenant that Jesus made between god and all mankind. By leaving the principles of the Doctrine of Christ by changing the doctrine of baptism, resurrection, eternal judgment or any other commands that are written in the new testament of Jesus Christ. When these very same Christian's have seen the power of God revealed to them when they have tasted of the fruits of the heavenly gift and were made partakers of the Holy Ghost. And they have tasted of the good word of God and the powers of the world to come. If they shall fall away to renew them again unto repentance; seeing they have crucified to themselves the son of God afresh and put him to an open shame. Now, these people have denied the faith, denied the power of the Holy Ghost, and denied the commandments of Jesus Christ and Jehovah God, thereby, they have denied the Faith.

There is an example of a man who committed the unforgivable sin against the Holy Ghost. This man was one of Jesus Disciples, whose name was Judas. This man was one of the twelve disciples that Jesus chose at the beginning of his ministry. So Judas was with Jesus, day and night for three years, and he witnessed the miracles that Jesus performed by the power of the Holy Ghost that lived in Jesus' body all during his ministry. So Judas both saw and tasted of the divine power of the Holy Ghost by the miracles that Jesus has done before his very eyes. Then Judas allowed Satan to enter into his body when He went to the evil Pharisees and betrayed Jesus for thirty pieces of silver.

Then the Pharisees put Jesus through a mocking trial, loaded with false witnesses and when Judas, his betrayer, seeing that Jesus was condemned, was remorseful and tried to repent. But Judas had committed the blasphemy against the Holy Ghost and there is never forgiveness for this sin in this world or in the world to come.

Can a person commit the unforgivable sin of blasphemy against the Holy Ghost before they become a Christian? There is a great example of this very thing in the Scriptures, by a man named Saul. Saul was a Pharisee and He was a doctor of the Law of Moses. Saul did not believe in Jesus when Jesus worked three years in his ministry until Jesus was hung on the Cross, and when he was buried, Jesus rose from the dead, spending forty days and nights with the apostles and then he ascended back into heaven. Now Saul was still a persecutor of the Christians, even murdering some and putting some in prison. But when Jesus appeared to Saul on the road to Damascus as Saul was going down to arrest Christian's and bring them back to Jerusalem for trial. Jesus converted Saul from the Jewish religion to Christianity and Saul changed his name to Apostle Paul becoming a great servant of the Lord Jesus Christ. Paul said that He was a blasphemer and the chief of all sinners, but Jesus had mercy and enabled Him to become an apostle, putting Him in the ministry. He obtained mercy because He did it ignorantly in unbelief. This proves that a person cannot commit any kind of sin that God won't forgive them before they become a Christian. This makes the Invitation from Jehovah God true; the spirit which is God and Christ Spirit and the bride which is the church, say come and let all that heareth by obeying the words written in the Bible, say, "Come. And let him that is athirst come, and whosoever will let them take of the waters of life freely."

The key of wisdom to understanding how Christians can avoid committing blasphemy against the Holy Ghost is on this wise. Believe every word written in the Holy Scriptures as they are the oracles from his mouth to all mankind which tell us we can't be regenerated from a sinful person to a righteous person without the help of the Holy Spirit. The Holy Spirit is given to every Christian at baptism to live in their bodies, to guide and lead them and He will teach you the Scriptures. The Holy Spirit is our witness to God and Christ of our every word, and deed that we commit upon this earth. He will justify or condemn us in the day of our judgment before Jesus Christ, whom God has appointed as the supreme judge of all mankind. If you die and the Holy Spirit does not live in your body, you will be lost eternally, because we must have the spirit of God who raised Jesus from the dead, living in our bodies to raise us up from the dead to be saved eternally. We can be forgiven of every sin that we can commit against God and Christ and be forgiven, but we cannot be forgiven of the sin against the Holy Ghost. This is why Jehovah God warns everyone not to grieve the Holy Ghost, do not quench him by putting him out of your life through your unbelief, do not resist the help of the Holy Ghost. The Holy Ghost will not live in the sinners and ungodly people, only the Christians who obey God's words.

Epilogue

I testify before heaven and earth that these things are true. The short version of these two great encounters with my Living Jehovah God and my guardian angel was in 1950 and again in 2011. When I was seven years old, sick unto death, and no one upon the earth could save me from death. As I lay on my death bed in the cold winter of 1950, crying rivers of tears. I remembered the Bible teachings of my Christian mother, and I believed 100% in God and I loved Him because He took the beggar man to paradise and God through the rich man in hell. I thought what a great God for loving the beggar because we were poor also. I was down to the end of my rope of life, and I remembered my God, so I prayed to Him three times and made a deal with God. God heard my silent prayers and had my guardian angel speak to me from heaven and God sent Him to heal me of chicken pox, measles, and mumps with a temperature of 106 degrees. And the angel showed me in a vision the Lake of Fire that will come upon the earth at the end of the last judgment.

On the second visit, God sent the very same angel from heaven to visit with me, and when I talked to the angel, God heard me and God told the angel what to say to me and I communicated with God and Jesus Christ for about thirty minutes. God chastised me for my sins and giving God credit for the unlawful pleasures of sin in my life. As I began crying, I repented of all these sins and God forgave me of them, also forgave me of two sins that I had committed since I was baptized at the age of 40 years old. God said through the angel since I had repented of my sins, He also was forgiving me of the sin that I worried about from time to time and the sin that He doesn't think that I knew it was a sin to commit. And He was writing my name back into the book of life, himself and my name would never be removed again. Now no one upon the earth knew about these sins, except the ones that I committed them with, I kept them secret; but God knew my entire life, as a prodigal son, committing sins and knew my every thought.

Now the things that I learned of our living Jehovah God are wonderful. I learned that He loves those who believe and love Him very deeply, and I learned that His heart is full of love and mercy, forgiving us of our sins when we repent of them. As I stood before the angel, it was as if I was standing before God and I learned that He knew my entire life, He said He was so happy the day I was baptized into the kingdom at age forty and now I am seventy-five years old. I learned that children really have guardian angels like Jesus Christ told us. And I learned how God still works through His holy angels today on earth. I learned that God stores up every prayer that is prayed unto Him as a memorial to every one of us who pray to Him, and He hears every prayer of the righteous or sinners or ungodly persons; but He only answers those of the righteous or the repentant prayers. I learned that we are saved by grace, but we are judged by our works and He will extend some grace to those who are repentant of their sins as He done for me. The very last question that God asked me through the angel, which said to me, "Jerry, God wants to ask you a question if he could?" and I said, "Yes and I will answer the question if I can."

The angel said, "Jerry, Jesus wants God to ask you if you love Him?"

"Well," I said, "Lord God, yes, I love Him, seeing how that I am a gentile and we were without a covenant relationship with God until Jesus came and died on the cross for our sins and a new covenant, whereby I can be saved."

God said Jerry that was a good answer. As I pondered this in my heart, about two weeks later, I knew why He asked such a question. Jesus wanted me to know if you love me, keep my commandments and never sin anymore!

9 781645 752592